Out Of Ruins
Healing after Adultery

LAURA SAMUELSON

CrossBooks™
A Division of LifeWay
1663 Liberty Drive
Bloomington, IN 47403
www.crossbooks.com
Phone: 1-866-879-0502

©2011 Laura Samuelson. All rights reserved.

No part of this book may be reproduced, stored in a retrieval system, or transmitted by any means without the written permission of the author.

First published by CrossBooks 09/09/2011

ISBN: 978-1-4627-0590-0 (sc)
ISBN: 978-1-4627-0591-7 (hc)

Scripture taken from the Holy Bible, New International Version®. Copyright © 1973, 1978, 1984 Biblica. Used by permission of Zondervan. All rights reserved.

Scripture quotations taken from the New American Standard Bible®, Copyright © 1960, 1962, 1963, 1968, 1971, 1972, 1973, 1975, 1977, 1995 by The Lockman Foundation. Used by permission." (www.Lockman.org)

Scripture taken from the King James Version of the Bible.

Printed in the United States of America
\This book is printed on acid-free paper.

Any people depicted in stock imagery provided by Thinkstock are models, and such images are being used for illustrative purposes only.

Certain stock imagery © Thinkstock.

Because of the dynamic nature of the Internet, any web addresses or links contained in this book may have changed since publication and may no longer be valid. The views expressed in this work are solely those of the author and do not necessarily reflect the views of the publisher, and the publisher hereby disclaims any responsibility for them.

Contents

FOREWORD VII
PREFACE XI
OUR STORY 1
WHAT NOW? 7
HOW MUCH DETAIL SHOULD I KNOW? 13
ENDING THE RELATIONSHIP AND BREAKING THE TIE . . 17
OPEN HEART 21
BREAKING THE CYCLE OF DECEPTION 23
AFTER THE DUST SETTLED 27
A TOUGH LESSON 33
NOT TAKING ADVANTAGE 37
RETURNING TO INTIMACY 41
THE "OCTOPUS" OF WOUNDING 45
WISDOM IN KNOWING WHEN TO SHARE 49
CREATING A GOOD HABIT 55
UNDERSTANDING PAIN FROM ANOTHER ANGLE 61
RETURNING TO MINISTRY 65
WHAT IF THERE IS NO REPENTANCE? 69
ARE WE SURVIVORS? 73
CONCLUSION 77
ACKNOWLEDGMENTS 103

FOREWORD

There are times and events where you make a choice, that affects the rest of your life in irreversible ways. The decisions regarding relationship may be one of the most dwelt upon, reflected upon, and regretted.

Extra-marital relationships can be the most devastating of all. As Laura and I can attest, the stress and strain of an affair on a marriage is one of the most difficult of situations a husband and wife can endure. A sickness, deformity, or death does not have an identifiable adversary. Yet, an affair occurs at the choice of a spouse and believed confidant; hence, the ability to forgive and forget is not an easy choice. It is seldom a choice considered. In this day and age, the lack of gravity in the marriage vows leads to the easy decision to divorce and walk away, rather than walk the tough path toward restoration. RESTORATION? Yes, restoration of the relationship that you chose to make at the exchange of your vows, "Until death do us part."

The concept of adulterous thoughts to be with someone other than your spouse is not new. In <u>Gone With the Wind,</u> Scarlett made her choices, not on what was best for her or her family, but upon what would fuel her adulterous desires to be close to the one she wanted. The desire for someone else is portrayed and expounded upon in novels, movies, soap operas, magazine articles, etc. After the prominent figure in the story gets, and wins the heart of the one they long for, the observer is made to feel that all is now right with the world. But, never revealed from the stories that we see portrayed, is how a spouse recovers or saves their relationship after an affair. What we see and accept is separation, unforgiveness, divorce, hate, and the destruction of several lives: husband, wife, children, parents, friends . . . The list is long and restoration is non-existent.

Once the first step toward an adulterous affair is begun, even mentally, each following step can be easier to accept. As the adulterous path gets longer, the ability to turn back and work to restore what was left behind becomes more and more difficult; and less and less foreseeable. How can you turn away from what now "feels" good, and turn toward what is going to be a hard and possibly unattainable restoration?

Where are the stories that give us hope? Where are the heroes that have won the unbeatable battles? When we look around us, we usually find those that have walked away from the battle to give us advice. Most often, that advice does not lean toward restoration and healing. Healing? Yes, healing and renewal! It *is* possible!

With work and determination, your relationship can be restored, not only to what it was before, but to something better. Do not be misled to believe that the restoration comes easily; it does not. If it helps, let's consider the restoration of an automobile. When new and in its prime, it was a sleek, desirable mode of transportation. But after it has deteriorated with rust and time, we accept the amount of work and determination required to restore it. Why is it, that we can understand that type of restoration requirement towards a car, but not towards a relationship? An apology and change of heart might heal a broken relationship right away, but if it does not meet that anticipation – we want to just walk away.

To restore a relationship takes time, determination, and patience. To reacquire what is important, we must approach the goal with a selfless determination. The relationship is what is important, not you! You have to choose to do what is needed to achieve the prize. Before the wedding you pursued the prize with selfless actions. You must resort to the same tactics. In the Bible, Paul, a great apostle and leader among the first followers of Jesus wrote in I Corinthians 9:24 "Know ye not that they which run in a race run all, but one receiveth the prize? So run, that ye may obtain." (NIV) Paul was speaking about doing what it takes to reach the desired results.

By picking up this book you have begun the race to win back what was taken from you, whether that was your spouse, your relationship, your intimacy, the innocence of the union, or the ability to be completely transparent with your spouse. Your marriage is worth the battle. Winning the battle for your marriage (not for you) is the prize. Run this race with determination and tenacity. The prize is worth it.

May God bless and hold you up as you fight for your marriage.

Glen

P.S. Remember, the enemy of your marriage does not want you to win and will do all he can to persuade you to give up. God is on your side and restoration is His desire. Ask Him for help and fortitude as you fight, and request that His angels fight with you for victory. There is no warrior bigger than God!

PREFACE

There are many husbands and wives who spend a great deal of time worrying and suspecting their spouses of infidelity. Some have good reason to suspect, and others waste a hefty chunk of their lives getting all worked up for nothing. I was not either of those. I spent no time on suspicions, and if on rare occasion, the fleeting thoughts of doubt crossed my mind, I would rebuke the devil for intruding on my peace.

Both of us were Christians when we married. We had several ministries in our local church and community. We thought we were immune from so many problems of the unsaved around us. Our goal was to live together and raise our children as happily as we could while serving God.

It doesn't really matter who knows or who doesn't before a revelation of adultery occurs, the heavy weight of reality still hits like an earth shattering wrecking ball into our hearts and homes. I remember thinking that a bullet would have been more merciful. I am about to share with you a very personal and honest story of the walk to healing that my husband and I experienced. It is a level of openness that we both agreed on, with the intent to help any who find themselves in the heap of marital ruins that we found ourselves in. We had ministered to couples for many years, but in the midst of that marriage ministry, we crashed into a wall of deceit and pain that literally brought us to our knees.

What I thought was a firm foundation of a Christian home, suddenly, and with just a few words, became a piece of wreckage that seemed to have too many gaping holes for me to know where to safely stand. The only truth that I knew for sure was the strength of my relationship with God. It was from that one constant and faithful truth that I began to draw. From within the first few seconds of my emotional floor being pulled out from under me, I began asking the Holy Spirit, my Faithful Friend, what to do.

God gently and specifically gave me steps that I felt were a direct "map" of how to walk on a solid pathway out of despair, and onto a road that led to healing. I had no idea at the time that I would someday rejoice in the journey. No, not rejoice in the sin, but in the victory.

My husband and I are closer and more in love now than I ever could have imagined, even before the adultery. I have learned from the Holy Spirit that infidelity wasn't the only problem; it was a symptom of a deeper heart condition.

This is such a personal issue, and it carries so deep a wound, that it is difficult to talk about even among friends. The effects of sexual sin bring shame not only to the offender, but even to the one who has been "cheated on". That shame tends to silence even the successful couples. Once out of the rubble, who wants to go back into it, even if only in memory?

I wanted to find someone who had not only walked through it, but someone who had received victory on the other side of the pain. Finding that person was next to impossible. I knew only a handful and they weren't all that anxious to share the nitty-gritty of what they went through. God did give us special people to help us through those first few months. We found couples who wanted to see both of us restored, but most of them had not walked through adultery. We really wanted some practical steps from couples who knew what we knew and had felt what we were feeling.

If I were to embark on a journey through a dark forest filled with danger, I would tend to look for those who had not only studied the forest, but successfully maneuvered their way through to safety. I would ask for their knowledge of known traps and escape routes. My uneasiness would be helped by hearing their stories of victory. So, here is our ugly truth, with the desire to make your journey through this forest a little less intimidating.

I never would have chosen to walk this route. The repulsive thought of it was too scary to even toy with. I hurt for those I had seen walk it before me, but it was too vast and dark to imagine walking through myself. Unfortunately, we don't always get to choose which paths we will take. When we are married, we also get to walk through the decisions of our spouse. Our choice then, is how we will respond to the road we discover we are already standing on.

The wonderful thing is that our chosen response decides where we will end up; and ultimately what kind of shape we will be in when it's over. That is something we can determine for ourselves.

We may not have control over where we find ourselves, but we can control whether or not we will shame ourselves in the midst of it. We can determine that reacting to sheer emotions will be squelched and placed second to choosing an honorable response. That is in our hands. It's not the first choice in our nature, but it's definitely our decision to make.

We can also retrace our steps when we find our reactions have led us down a wrong turn. No person is perfect. Many steps my husband and I took had to be retraced and started over. The beauty found in desperation was that we were not alone. God truly instructed us when we asked for his guidance.

I am writing this so it will help those who need to hear a positive testimony. I am penning our story for those who find the same difficulty in locating couples who have fought this battle successfully. We don't carry a license to practice counseling. We are not doctors of philosophy. What we do offer is our story. As you read this, I will try to describe the steps and road map that God took us through.

Every story is different with surrounding circumstances, but we are not so different in our pain. God's scripture applies to all of us, from every walk of life. As you begin your own journey to healing, we encourage you to seek the help of your pastor, your counselor, or someone you trust to instruct you in God's Biblical truth that will bring you life, healing and hope.

Renewal is a process. God wants to give you the tools to help make this process as clear as possible. It is my hope that you can glean from our journey, the fruit of hope. Hope for life, better than what it has ever been before. Hope that in spite of immense anguish, pain and anger, a beautiful pearl can arise out of the shell of turmoil.

My husband and I, in working with couples for over twenty years, have seen many different stories. The exciting thing is that every couple who surrenders themselves to God's scriptural principles gets healed. His truth never fails.

Revelation 12:11 (KJV) says: "And they overcame him by the blood of the Lamb, and the word of their testimony…." It is this testimony that I would like to share, not to expose my husband's sin or to glory in our sufferings, but to tell of the restorative power of the Lord Jesus Christ. Here is the map to freedom that He gave us. May it bless your heart, and may it bless your marriage.

Laura

OUR STORY

The night began so wonderfully. I had just dropped off our three boys at a children's church function and my husband and I would be home with just our eleven month old daughter. It was two weeks before Christmas 1996 and the house was decorated with shiny lights, tinsel, stockings hanging on the fire place mantle, and a decorated Christmas tree in the corner.

When I returned from dropping off the boys, I saw Glen had built a fire in the fireplace and had made me a surprise dinner. I am usually the cook in the home, so I knew he was planning an especially romantic evening.

We visited while we ate a quiet dinner and enjoyed the peaceful Christmas music Glen had turned on for the "mood" of the evening. While enjoying this special time together with three little ones away, my thoughts were interrupted by a fairly loud voice saying "he has been with another woman." It wasn't an accusing voice. It was very matter-of-fact and it came out of nowhere. This thought had only crossed my mind once or twice before, and those times had been more of an "I wonder what I would ever do if …" sort of thought. The voice I was hearing now was different though. This was a definite supernatural voice. Even though I had heard the voice of the Holy Spirit before, I quickly determined in my mind that this was a trick of the devil trying to spoil our wonderful time together. I rebuked the thought and shoved it aside like I was shaking off a wasp from my arm.

Later in the evening, we were lying in front of the fireplace when the phone rang. I got up and answered it. The voice on the other end was a man's and he asked to talk to Glen. I handed Glen the phone in the kitchen and began doing dishes while they spoke. We didn't have a cordless phone at the time, so he was standing just a few feet away from me. I was only vaguely listening until I noticed Glen all but hiding in the corner, talking in a hushed tone. I tuned in enough to hear him saying to the man "No, I have a good marriage. There's nothing like that happening." Obviously, I began really listening at that point.

When Glen hung up I asked him what the call was about. He told me a distant friend was suspicious of the relationship Glen had with his wife. When I asked for more information, Glen told me that they had held hands once while he was away from home. I began to feel shaky and sick. Why would he hold someone's hand? What was the story behind that? I was too stunned to ask. I put our daughter to bed, and later put the boys to bed after they arrived home. Holding hands with someone else's wife was devastating itself, but the same voice that had spoken to me earlier that evening was telling me there was more.

I tried to process the fact that he had been gone, and somehow ended up holding another woman's hand. There was no situation I could envision that would allow for that, other than a romantic one. What in the world was he thinking? Why would he dismiss that phone call and simply say he had held hands with her? I wanted to know what had happened, but then again, perhaps I really didn't want to know. I certainly was not going to just let things rest with, "We held hands once."

I felt like I was standing in a dark room with a huge shadow looming in front of me. It seemed there was a dark and present danger right in the middle of my marriage, but I hoped with all of my heart that there was a reasonable explanation for what had happened. My mind searched frantically for any reason that Glen might think was appropriate to hold this woman's hand. Maybe they were walking and he helped her up a steep hill; but why would he be walking with her? She was an old girlfriend, maybe he meant they held hands when they were young. That would explain why he didn't seem to think it was a big deal.

When we go to bed at night, I usually put my head on Glen's chest until I drift off to sleep. As we lay in bed that night after the children were asleep, I once again had my head there. Not looking Glen in the face gave me courage to ask him once again. (He later told me he wanted to wait until the kids were in bed before sharing the whole truth.)

I loved him so much, and I wanted to believe the best in him. I tried to draw comfort from the warmth of my face resting on his chest. Surely this handholding was an oversight of judgment, a one time accident or a thing from way in the past. Why would her husband call though? What triggered that suspicion? Had Glen really been so lonely while he was away from home that he replaced me and our marriage with a blast from the past? That voice that I heard earlier, was that God telling me something had happened? I knew there would be no rest in my heart until I asked, but I was afraid to know. What if he had really spent time with her and they had ended up holding hands and rekindled some old feelings?

Surely he would have enough sense to know that was wrong. Glen was a very sensible man. He had four children and a wife. He would never spend time with someone else. He knew the danger that would create. He had just surprised me with a wonderful dinner and a romantic evening. Why would anyone go to that trouble if his heart was divided?

He had been especially solemn since the phone call, so I asked him if he was alright. He said no, he wasn't alright, and we needed to talk. I asked if it was about the call and looked at him. He shook his head yes. I put my head back down and waited. When he didn't say anything, I asked if they had done more than hold hands. He again said "Yes." I had not dared to let myself think of the worst possible scenario. It felt like a knife was slowly invading my chest headed for my heart. It took a minute to draw up the courage, but finally I asked if they had slept together, and he said "Yes." There it was; the cold knife blade pierced my heart like a death blow. I felt like a heavy wet blanket of grief began to crawl up my entire body from the bottoms of my feet to the top of my head. Then I asked "More than once?" and again he responded, "Yes." Now the blade twisted and every reality I knew was suddenly distorted. This happened more than once? It was big, ugly, and incomprehensive.

He said he had been trying to find a way to tell me but hadn't come up with one. The phone call that night had been from her husband. He had learned about Glen's ongoing relationship with his wife, and had given Glen until morning to tell me.

There is no way to explain the feeling that came over me. It was a spirit, soul and body pain all at the same time. I started to get up, but that familiar voice told me not to move yet. I asked a few more questions and tried to absorb the bitterness of it all and prayed at the same time for help. It was hard to even know what to ask. The whole thing seemed surreal. I closed my eyes and thought "God, you had to know about this." As the shock settled in, I told Glen that I was going to the bathroom, but I'd be back.

I thought I was going to throw up as I sat in the bathroom. My stomach twisted in knots, and my head felt like moss had grown around it. What had he done? How was this possible? Was this some kind of sick joke? I wanted to die, to disappear, whatever it took to be away from this wretched stench. Then the voice came again. "He who calls on the name of the Lord shall be saved. Call on me."

I knew I needed saved from the pit I felt myself sliding into. I began saying "Jesus, Jesus, Jesus, Jesus" over and over; I'm not sure how many times. It was as if every time I spoke the name of Jesus I was begging for help, but at the same time, I was yielding to Him. He knew what to do. He wasn't shocked. He would be my coach, by my own choice, and I knew He was trustworthy.

When the bulk of nausea passed, the voice said "Go back to bed and put your head back on his chest." It was as clear as if God were standing right in front of me.

"But how?" I asked.

"Go back." He said once again. It was a gentle voice, but very unswerving.

I obeyed. I could think of a million things I would have rather done right then (including removing some of Glen's body parts), but God gave me the strength to do it. I forced myself to climb back into bed and I put my head back on his chest.

"Now what do I do?" I asked.

"Forgive him." God spoke so directly and so clear.

"Now?"

"Yes, now."

I certainly didn't feel like forgiving, but I heard myself say as I yielded to God's direction: "The first thing I need to do is forgive you."

I knew God was right. This thing was too big and too ugly to hold on to for any length of time; so we prayed. I told God I forgave Glen, and I told Glen I forgave him. It was powerful. It didn't have much feeling, but it was intense and decisive, simply obedience. Was it easy? No! But it was like I had given God control in that bathroom and He was orchestrating every second and every move. I felt like a robot as I put myself in automatic and simply obeyed the voice of the Holy Spirit as he instructed me.

Glen asked what we should do from there; then he asked if I wanted a divorce. I thought about our four children and tried to comprehend the depth of pain they would experience. I knew that the best hope for their lives was to have our family intact, so I said I didn't want a divorce. I was still trying to comprehend how we had gone from a romantic dinner a few hours ago, to talking about divorce. We never used that word in our conversations; not even in jest. This was Scriptural grounds for divorce. No question about that, but God allows for it, He doesn't require it. I could not see, in light of the cross, dumping everything we'd built and choosing a sentence of death for our home.

This was not a choice to ignore what had happened though. I told Glen that I was a bad faker. My parents, siblings and close friends would have to know what was happening, because I wouldn't put on a fake face in front of them. It was somewhere between one and three o'clock in the morning, but we picked up the phone and called a couple who were close friends of ours.

Their response was a loving one. They said they had known this was happening for over a year. God had shown them and asked them to pray for us. Wow! God had shown them?

God knew the path we would have to walk down. I was amazed that He had begun preparing the way, long before I ever imagined the journey. This wasn't a surprise to God. He knew both Glen and me well. He knew my needs before I did, and He was indeed directing our path.

I was reminded of the Proverbs 3:5-6 passage. "Trust in the Lord with all thine heart; and lean not unto thine own understanding. In all thy ways acknowledge Him and He shall direct thy paths." (KJV)

The next several hours of that night were awful. We went back to bed together and tried to sleep, but the sleep was not restful, and I'd find myself waking up already sobbing. I wept like that for several nights following, but there was a peace in the midst of that storm, knowing that God was in control.

We had no idea what couples who went through this were supposed to do. Were we supposed to talk? Should we separate? What should we say? There certainly wasn't a manual for this sort of thing that I knew of, but the Lord was there. He was teaching us minute by minute what we were supposed to do. He knows me, and He knows Glen, and He knew just what we needed every step of the way.

"Now unto Him who is able to do exceeding abundantly beyond all that we ask or think, according to the power that works within us, to Him be the glory in the church and in Christ Jesus to all generations forever and ever. Amen." Ephesians 3:20-21 (NAS)

WHAT NOW?

As morning came, we prepared to go to my parent's home. We called them and asked if we could see them before they left for work. My dad is a pastor and my mom was the principal at the Christian school in our church, where they had served together for almost forty years.

They agreed to meet, and as we sat in their living room, Glen's honesty surprised me while he poured out the truth. My parents amazed me as they listened with understanding and love. If it had been my daughter, I probably would have gone for blood; but they refrained from any form of judgment and held their words from the vicious response I know had to be tempting.

Glen did most of the talking and confessed the entire truth to them. It had been a three year relationship with the other person. He shared that he had wanted to get out of it for some time, but wasn't sure how. He certainly didn't have the option of talking to his pastor, since the pastor was my dad.

I began to see a glimpse of the trap he had been in, but at the same time the feelings of betrayal were terribly overpowering. Again and again I kept repeating to myself "I forgive him. I forgive him."

I barely remember what was spoken with my parents other than that they loved us both and wanted to help us wherever possible. We told them that we would have to step down as praise and worship leaders and teachers in the church. My dad and mom were dealing with their own emotions at the time, but managed to show love to Glen in spite of the circumstances.

As wounded as my heart was, I was moved by Glen's honesty and repentant heart.

Before we left, my dad gave us a wonderful, life giving piece of advice that I would now recommend to anyone in a difficult situation like this. He said he would release us from our responsibilities at the church, but only with the agreement that we set a date as to when we would return. He told us that it was important to have a goal to work toward. We prayed and agreed together that we would work to return to our positions in five months. Although we can't limit God or determine when we can heal, I felt that we had a lifeline of normality thrown to us. Of course our lives would never be the same, but it was a goal to strive for.

I thought things were going pretty well for what we were dealing with. I was being obedient and staying on top of the forgiveness thing, but then pride does go before a fall doesn't it? (Proverbs 16:18) When Glen left for work, I fell hard.

Soon after he left, the phone rang and it was the husband of the other woman. He asked if Glen had told me the truth and began sharing how he had pieced things together to discover it for himself. More and more came out: how he'd found a post office box in their name so they could send things to each other; phone records that showed they were talking to each other regularly on the phone in Glen's office; a package of sexy underwear she had wrapped up for him but had not sent yet, and many other details of their three-year relationship, I began to realize that this wasn't just a one-night stand that had gotten out of control in the heat of the moment. It was a planned and very well thought out web of deception that was wound into more of our lives than I could have ever thought.

Learning that Glen had been talking to her on the phone regularly seemed to be more painful to me than the physical betrayal. There was a soul attachment and emotional bond as well. Was he in love with her? A secret post office box that "they" could use……..? How was there a "they" that I knew nothing about? It was too much to wrap my brain around.

I had enough of God's grace pouring over me to be able to encourage the husband that God wanted to see both of our marriages healed. I prayed with him that the healing power of Jesus would restore their family and help them walk through this successfully. I don't think either one of them knew Jesus personally, but I wanted to throw him the same lifeline I was able to hold on to. God was helping us so much, and I couldn't imagine going through this without Him. Isaiah 41:13 (KJV) tells us "For I the Lord thy God will hold thy right hand, saying unto thee, Fear not; I will help thee." Why would anyone want to climb out of a pit without the very hand of God, when He offers it so graciously?

I hung up the phone with the other woman's husband and sat with my head in my hands. I remembered that just a few months back, Glen had asked me not to call him so much at work. His boss had told him he was spending too much time on the phone. I realized that it wasn't because of my calls to my husband. It was because he was talking to both me and this other woman, and spending too much time between both of us…And I was the one Glen asked to cut down on the calls.

All of a sudden, I shifted from shock and grief to boiling anger and hurt. He had asked me not to call him as much. Had he asked her to refrain as well? All of the experiences that had happened in our lives in the past three years seemed to cheapen and become repulsive and counterfeit. I thought of all the milestones we had celebrated together. Anniversaries, birthdays, holidays, the conception and birth of our long hoped-for daughter, all happened during their affair. (I hate that word "affair." It sounds so happy. This was definitely not happy.)

As the reality of it all, and the anger soaked in, I slumped to the floor and began to sob uncontrollably. I cried hard and began asking God why. What had I done wrong? Shame covered me like a thick cloud. I began to picture everything ugly about myself that may have driven Glen to this other woman. I was over my ideal weight at the time. Was it that? I certainly don't fit the bill for a beauty queen. My clothes are simple and far from extravagant or sexy. I'm not very daring when it comes to public expressions of our sexuality. I felt "used up," old fashioned, and unexciting. I saw that as a long term wife, there was much wanting in my inventory. I realized that I was plain and undesirable to Glen, and for the first time in my life, unworthiness crept over me so strongly that it made me want to hide from everyone and everything.

I pleaded with God to help me from deep within my spirit. I could hear my own voice groaning out cries that were foreign to me. My sobs sounded like another person's voice. Reality seemed so vague that I felt like I'd entered someone else's life.

It was about that time that my sister came over and said she had spoken to our parents. She had come to take our children for the day. What a blessing! I was so overwhelmed at that point that I had completely forgotten them playing in the other room. I was once again touched by God's grace. He had sent angels to entertain them, and they had been completely distracted in another room, content and quiet. This was four children under the age of ten, and one of them not even a year old yet. God's care of both them, and me, still touches my heart.

After my sister left with the kids I began cleaning the house. That's usually what I do when I get really angry. It lets off a lot of steam in a positive way. My family sometimes teases me when the house gets cluttered, that it's time to get mom angry again. I cleaned like crazy for just a few minutes, but this anger was completely different. It was a paralyzing sense of devastation. Before long I was on the floor again with a broom and dustpan in my hands, bawling like a dam had burst.

Then as I sat there, I realized that I had no idea what diseases that woman may have had. I thought of my children and wondered if my now contaminated body might have passed something on to them. I was still nursing our daughter and dreaded that she might suffer from a sexually transmitted disease. I hurried to the shower and began to scrub myself as I sobbed through gritted teeth. I wanted every trace of that woman off of me. I've probably never been so clean. I sank to the floor and stayed there long after the hot water ran out. I knew I was getting frantic and felt as if I were going over some abstract edge. I remember my spirit commanding my soul to, "Get it together!"

The shower is my personal prayer closet, so once again I cried out to God and asked him to keep me sane. The verse from 2 Timothy 1:7 (KJV), "For God hath not given us the spirit of fear; but of power and of love, and of a SOUND MIND." began comforting me immediately. I could feel God's gentle presence begin to take control. I clung on to the "sound mind" part as I prayed. God was more real to me, and the Holy Spirit more awesome a counselor, than any other tangible person in my life. There simply is no human being who can comfort in that same deeply peaceful and healing way as Jesus can.

He pulled me back together and helped me climb out of that shower. He gently spoke to me that I was already washed with His blood. I was clean, because He has made me white as snow. His blood could cleanse deeper than any soap and water I could ever use. Jesus knew just what I needed to hear, and His words comforted me in my need.

HOW MUCH DETAIL SHOULD I KNOW?

I wish I could say that I went from a basket case to a sweet wife of incredible stature, but I simply went from a basket case back to an angry woman. I felt somewhat guilty for being angry, but God reminded me that it wasn't a sin to be angry. He said "Be ye angry, and sin not…" (Ephesians 4:26 NAS)

I was thankful that God allowed me the emotion that He had created in the first place. I didn't have to fake it with Him. There is a time to be angry; there is a time for mourning; there is a time to refrain from embracing. Ecclesiastes chapter three gave me permission to grieve. I just had to be wise not to take some of those verses literally, you know; a time to kill; a time to throw stones.

Just as I was coming out of that shower the phone rang. It was Glen.

"How are you doing?" He asked in a concerned voice.

"Not so good," I honestly replied.

I told him I was very angry, and I had a lot of questions I needed answered.

Over the past 12 years of marriage, up to that point, there had been little confessions of "smaller" infractions. There were things that couldn't officially be called "adultery," but they had crossed the line of purity. I told him I was done with the little confessions. I wanted to know all of the truth out in the open right now. I wanted to know every incident of sexual sin and betrayal. If all things were out on the table, I could quit wondering what else I didn't know. I could deal with it in a lump sum and not have any more patterns of "wound and heal, wound and heal."

He immediately came home from work, and for the next few hours we sat in the living room while he told me everything I wanted to know. We retraced the years of his life, his childhood, his dating years, time I was away at college during our engagement, and the entire time we were married.

I was shocked at all the things he had been hiding. I fought the temptation to give in to my thoughts that I'd married a genuine pervert. I wanted to pass judgment and slam down the gavel, but at the same time I appreciated the openness and honesty that he offered at the risk of judgment.

I quietly prayed and asked the Lord for wisdom. Then I proceeded to ask in detail in what specific things he and this other woman had participated. I wanted to be careful not to get myself all worked up over details. I knew if we were to ever have complete openness between us, I needed to be able to respond to him physically without always wondering if he had "done this with another woman." Genesis says that Adam and Eve were naked and unashamed. I had sought that intimacy for years. If there remained hidden sin between us, I just didn't see how that complete purity was possible.

I, in turn, confessed to him in detail all of the ways I had crossed the line in my dating years. Although Glen is the only man I have "been with" and I had been faithful since marriage, I knew I had sinned in my dating years with excessive kissing and fondling. I also struggled in my thought life wondering if I would have been happier had I married someone else. I compared Glen to other men, not so much in looks, but in personalities. I was attracted to men who portrayed purity and godliness, because I desired a man like that so much. It was only fair to admit my own sin, and I wanted a clean slate going both ways.

We have had many couples ask us how much detail they should know from the offending spouse. My answer to them is, "How close do you want to be when you are on the other side of this hurdle?" Are you willing to keep obstacles in between you? When it's all said and done, will you still question in your heart? This is what I needed for me, complete openness.

I have talked to women who said they would suffer more if they had the detailed pictures in their minds. I believe that every person should ask the Holy Spirit to give wisdom as to how much they should know. God is the one who created us. He knows how much we can handle. I also know that much of the closeness that Glen and I now enjoy stems from the fact that there are no secrets between us.

What about the betrayer who says, "I don't want to hurt the other person?" Do we really believe that a sin covered up by deception or fear isn't already hurting the relationship? Hidden sin is like having a sticker bush between the two of you. Sometimes you know what it is, and other times you only identify that you just can't seem to completely connect with each other. For years, before I knew what was going on, I knew something wasn't right. I couldn't place my finger on it, but I knew something ugly was just under the surface. Sin is like that. It separates. Sin is what separated us from our heavenly Father. Marriage here on earth is a representation of our relationship with God. Sin, even when hidden, separates us from each other. It causes a rift that can only be crossed when the obstacle of sin is removed. Sure, we can exist in a relationship where sin is covered up. But who would want to do that when the relationship is only half of what it could be?

Timing, of course, is everything. We don't want to just jump in and dump on our spouse. We try to pray before confessing hidden sin to each other. Glen hadn't been given the opportunity to pray and ask God to prepare my heart. My choice to demand complete honesty was a risk I wanted to take. I wanted to know the magnitude of our marital wreckage up front. I was already so wounded that if he'd said he had been with a million women it would have been the same depth of hurt as the one woman. What I needed was a break in the cycle of deception, a stop to the lies. Glen was willing to step up to the plate and give me what I needed.

Now the choice was up to me. Would I resent his truthfulness, or would I hold it as ammunition against him whenever I needed an upper hand in conflict? I have to admit, the thought was appealing. Glen was making himself vulnerable to me. In reality, he was giving me a box of bullets that could have been used as a lethal weapon in my pistol of revenge against both him and our marriage. God's voice again was clear, "Vengeance is mine, not yours."

As a child I learned what damage a life of unforgiveness could cause. My dad, a pastor, would come home from counseling people and say "If they only knew what poison they were feeding themselves with such bitterness." I'm pretty visual and I hate and fear snakes. My dad once told me that holding unforgiveness was the same as holding a poisonous snake. The more I fed my bitterness, the more the snake would grow, until it would become too big for me to control. Harboring the viper was inviting sickness and death to strike at will.

Forgiveness was a choice, an act of my will; a decided action contrary to how I felt. Now facing the deep betrayal and wound of adultery, I envisioned a snake, larger than any I had looked at before. As I write this, I share with you that my decision to forgive wasn't because I'm so super spiritual that I leapt the hurdle of forgiveness with a single bound. It also wasn't that my self-esteem was so low that I didn't realize my own worth and the magnitude of what was done against me. I chose to forgive because that was the only way to choose life. I chose Life for myself, Life for my marriage, Life for my husband, and Life for our children. I chose Jesus.

John 14:6 (KJV) says in Jesus' words, "…I am the Way, the Truth, and the Life: no man cometh unto the Father, but by me." If I was going to follow Jesus' counsel, Life was the only way to go. It's not that emotions didn't come or the temptation to judge wasn't there. It's just that I knew that our hope came from the Lord, and I didn't want to do anything to hinder my relationship with Him. It would be foolish to disobey the one who was offering the exact help and counsel we needed.

When those emotions come, I verbally or inwardly remind myself that I choose to forgive on an ongoing basis. I'm certainly no better than Jesus. If Glen's repentance is good enough for Jesus, I have no choice but to accept it as good enough for me. Anything less would be placing myself, and my hurt, above the blood of Jesus. Refusal to forgive is, in fact, idolatry.

ENDING THE RELATIONSHIP AND BREAKING THE TIE

The following few days were, of course, difficult. Glen was now relieved from trying to hide and cover his tracks, but he realized that I was just beginning the process of sorting through everything. While he was feeling relief and an outlet to all the pressure that had been building, I was crushed by the weight of what had been going on.

I appreciate that he allowed me to express what I was feeling. He could see clearly the two opposite places we were in, and he did his best to reach out and close the gap. He followed through with everything I told him I needed. I remember the first night that he told me of the adultery. One of the things he said was that he was willing to do whatever it took to get us through this. He had already been looking for a way out of the relationship with the other woman. I felt blessed that by the time I learned of it, he was ready to get out.

The irony of much of our dilemma was that we had been teaching marriage classes for over five years at the time. We were city directors for a marriage ministry, with leadership couples underneath our authority. We knew we would have to meet with our state directors who were also very close friends of ours. We were fully aware that this would be the end of our ministry. The heavy weight of the responsibility we were about to drop in their laps made us both feel guilt and shame. Of all the things to be doing when adultery hit, we had to be in a marriage ministry. It was more hypocritical than anything I could imagine. The ugliness and embarrassment was almost unbearable.

As Glen confessed to our state directors what had happened, we were expecting a rejecting blow and braced for the worst. I sat on the opposite side of the couch from Glen with my arms crossed. I was angry that we were losing the ministry. We shared how sorry we were that they would have to do both their job and ours until they could find a replacement for us. To our shock, they told us that the ministry was not what their concern was at the moment. Both of them expressed to us that we were more important to them than the ministry was. The ministry stuff could be worked out later. They poured out love to both of us, and said their main concern was that we get the help we needed to move forward with God's call on our lives. They actually believed that God still had a call on our lives. I wish I could express to them how powerfully hope giving that was. God wasn't going to throw our ministry away. (Romans 11:29 says: "For the gifts and calling of God are without repentance." KJV) Wow! They promised that they wouldn't side with either of us (that was huge) and would help us walk out the healing that we both needed.

What an awesome sense of relief washed over us as we talked together. We knew that the ministry we had shared up to that point was over, but we also learned that we were not going to be thrown out like the trash. They knew we were called to minister to marriages. In spite of this horrible chasm between God's call and our current crisis, they still wanted to see us fulfill our destiny. These amazing people were, and are, true friends in every sense of the word.

Their other very wise suggestion was that when Glen broke off the relationship with "her", I was to be on the phone with him. This wasn't a very appealing thing to me at the time, but I knew it was the right thing. They told us it needed to be immediate, and it needed to be final.

The next day we called her after praying together for strength and wisdom. As soon as she answered the phone, Glen told her that I was on the line also. He let her know that I knew about their relationship, and he was going to work to bring our marriage back on track. He told her it was over, he was ending their relationship, and there would never be contact between them again. She cried about ending it, but apologized to me for what had happened. She assured me that Glen had never said anything bad about me during their entire time spent together.

As I listened to her voice, I felt God's Spirit of compassion come over me. I actually felt a love and concern for her welling up in my spirit. I told her that I forgave her, and that I hoped she would get the help she needed for her own marriage. My heart went out to her and her family. I realized that they would be trying to struggle through the same issues as we were, but without a relationship with The Counselor, The Holy Spirit who was helping us so immensely. I told her that God could heal them both and that Glen and I hoped their marriage would be restored. We hung up on good terms, wishing the best for each other. The possibility for future contact was broken, and the relationship was left with the bluntness of an ungodly soul bond (Genesis 34:1-8) being sliced away. Even though the conversation was blunt, there weren't any words spoken in anger that we would later feel a need to repent for. Even years later, as I think about their family, I have a genuine concern that they are doing well. It is truly my hope that they found the way of peace and their family is intact. God has given me a love for them, even though we have never spoken again. As we talked that day, and The Holy Spirit poured out His grace over us, I know it was a lasting grace. That phone call was one of the most supernatural experiences of my life. God's intervention in the whole situation is astounding to me. Feeling love and concern for the woman, who had invaded my intimate marriage relationship, can only be explained by the presence of God. His love for her was evident in the way He moved in my heart during that conversation. I'm so grateful for His supernatural power.

Matthew 10:19b-20 "…for it shall be given you in that same hour what ye shall speak. For it is not ye that speak, but the Spirit of your Father which speaketh in you." (KJV)

OPEN HEART

When Glen and I hung up from talking to this woman, we hugged each other and prayed again, thanking God for his help. Then, Glen said he had something else to confess. I started to get a little nervous, but I reminded myself that we had given each other permission to keep the slate clean. I nodded my head, and Glen told me that when "she" said Glen never spoke anything bad about me, she was lying. He confessed that he had spoken many things against me, and he wanted to be careful not to let any more lies and deception sneak back in. I was hurt that he had spoken bad things about me, but I was blessed that he wasn't going to let even a fraction of untruth come between us again.

He was being careful not to allow a wrong statement from that woman to bring false comfort to me. He showed me in that moment that he was choosing truth over his own comfort and protection, and it meant the world to me. I could have asked what things he had said, but I chose instead to focus on his desire to be honest.

He has amazed me time and time again with his careful attention to watch for little "white lies" and for things that even appear deceitful. Even after all these years, the careful watch for absolute truth in him has not worn off. Glen is usually a little harder to yield than I am, but once God shows him something, he holds on to it with a tenacious grasp. His consistency to stay within God's boundaries far surpasses my own.

I am learning, through Glen's newly found love for the truth, to become watchful for ways I exaggerate or lie to protect myself. I have often struggled to candy coat things so I will look better or to protect myself from consequences. God calls all sin "sin". He never specifies little sins or big sins. Exaggeration is sin. Adultery is sin. Gluttony is sin. Swearing is sin. Murder is sin. It is all classified as sin. Sometimes I judge myself by my intent to be a good person. Therefore, I dismiss my own sin as infractions worthy of excuse; but sin isn't worthy of anything but death. That is why we all need the forgiveness of Jesus. He is the only one who is worthy of an audience with the Father. We need Him to be our advocate, so eternal life can be given to us as a gift; and it is a gift. All we have to do is ask for it, and recognize that it is only through Jesus that we can be saved. He is so patient with us. He loves us even more than we could love ourselves. What an amazing thing to be so loved by the King of Kings and the Lord of Lords that the ruler of the whole universe made it possible for us to live with Him forever, if we only ask. Grace…..Mercy……Unconditional love…………no wonder He asks us to walk in forgiveness. That's the same area He already abides in. He just wants us to abide there with Him.

BREAKING THE CYCLE OF DECEPTION

The next step in breaking deception was for Glen to confess to our church body and ministry leaders. This is a much debated subject, but since we were in leadership, we were counseled to be up front with people rather than wait for the gossip train to carry the news. One of the strongholds of adultery is deception. Confessing openly to one another is an effective tool against deception that carries a blow of finality right into the heart of deceit. It also allowed people to see Glen's true repentance and my true forgiveness. Had we kept it "secret," there would have been too much left to assumption.

We didn't want to scare or confuse any congregation visitors, so we asked to speak to the adult Sunday school class that had most of the church leadership and active adult members in it.

We asked a couple who were dear friends of ours (the ones we called the night Glen confessed) to come and pray for us and for our congregation as we poured out our hearts. We felt vulnerable for ourselves and we also felt the vulnerability that we would be bringing to our church family. Having our friends there as prayer warriors gave us the confidence to say what we needed to say.

Glen shared with the church how he had built the relationship by first trying to help "her" in her own marriage. They had spent time alone, and it had crossed the line, eventually leading to a physical relationship.

He told them he understood that they would be hurt and angry, since we had been ministering to them the whole time in worship and teaching. He apologized to them through tears of true sorrow. I was able to share that God was very present and was guiding me through the process of forgiveness.

When we were done sharing, one of the men spoke up that he was in no place to judge, since he was not without sin in his life. He also thanked Glen for his honesty and walked over to him and gave him a big bear hug. Several other men began offering their support and forgiveness, and before long they were all surrounding us with love and encouragement. The men were great.

Most of the women were great too; but there were some who had experienced the same betrayal. They had a harder time offering instant understanding. I could see that those women had not fully recovered from what had happened to them years before, and it scared me. To think that I could be so affected by this adultery that I could be bitter years from now and unable to offer forgiveness to others was frightening. I later asked God to help me release not only Glen, but men in general from any judgment that would linger and scar. It seemed to me that the unforgiveness these women carried had done much more damage to them, than the adultery itself.

Since my dad had been a pastor there long before I was born, there were people who had held me when I was a baby, and watched me grow up. This was difficult for them, as they felt the urge to protect me and defend me against Glen. Those who came to me later expressing a desire to side with me had good intentions. I had to keep reminding myself that I didn't need protection from Glen. We both needed protection from our adversary, the devil.

It was such a small group who struggled to forgive; and such a huge percentage that opened their arms to both of us. We saw it as a testimony to God's mercy operating in His body of believers. Most people seemed to appreciate our honesty, were pulling for our healing, and expected to see us minister again.

The next group of people we had to face was the leadership who we had been in charge of in the marriage ministry. This was the hardest group to face. The positive response from our church family helped give us courage to face this group. We both felt like the betrayal would be extra bitter for them. These were the wonderful people we had trained to minister to hurting couples. Now we were a hurting couple. The shame fell over us in a terribly heavy way as we drove to the meeting. It got so heavy that we had to stop on the way just to encourage each other to go on. We even jokingly toyed with the idea of driving to Mexico or someplace else to get out of it.

Nervous and sick to our stomachs, we held hands and prayed for God to give us the words to speak, and somehow turn our defeat into victory. We apprehensively arrived, and our precious state leaders gave us the floor when the meeting started.

I remember crying as Glen shared. It wasn't because of what he had done to me. It was watching him walk out the discipline of the Lord. Repenting to a group he loved so much and had invested so much into was agonizing for him. I was actually thankful that I was the one wronged, and not the one in Glen's place. It wasn't that I didn't have "flash thoughts" along the line that he was suffering and getting what he deserved, it's just that I had chosen the way of forgiveness. I couldn't allow myself to dwell on vindictive thoughts if we were ever to heal. Glen struggled through the meeting, explaining what had happened and how he had chosen to continue to see this woman over and over again. His heart was truly broken as he wept out his confession to our shocked leadership couples.

After we stepped down from leadership, the state directors laid out a plan to the leaders of how the ministry would be run in our absence. I remember them saying that they didn't know how long it would take before we could serve in any capacity in the ministry, but that we were further along in less than two weeks than many couples were in two years. That encouraged both of us.

One of the men spoke up and said that while Glen was talking, he was convicted about his loyalty to his own wife. It hadn't been another woman, but he had put his job above his relationship with her and their children. He cried as he shared the conviction and repentance he was experiencing. The couples embraced both of us, offering their encouragement and support. It was another Holy Spirit moment of grace, forgiveness and love.

We didn't leave the meeting in the state of shame that we thought we would. We felt blessed to have such an awesome group of Christian believers to call friends. As we drove home we talked excitedly about the way God had moved each time we had shared, both in our church and in our marriage ministry.

God took a horrible situation and turned it into a lesson of commitment to those couples we cared so much about. He was able to step in and minister at the very moment we stepped out. Truly, He loves and cares for them much more than we do.

AFTER THE DUST SETTLED

We talked a lot over the next few weeks. I told Glen it would take a while before I felt like I could be intimate with him. I was still working acceptance out in my mind. It seemed like I would just get one item "conquered" and another would pop up.

I've always felt that God gives us an anesthesia when we go through a death, crisis or trauma. There's a numbness that clouds our minds and slowly lets us wake up as we are able to absorb it. Sometimes when we look back it seems like slow motion, or a dream of some kind. Then we begin to cope, and the sting is felt in how the event has altered our everyday lives.

After we went through confession and repentance, we were without any ministry. We had spent hours of every day serving the Lord in some capacity. Now we were left with ourselves, and we were not in the best of shape. It was much easier to help other marriages than to whittle away the mountain of faults in our own.

The sting of reality was painfully strong. I struggled with the fact that I was being punished for something I didn't do. Every area of ministry and every social aspect of our lives were affected, and I hadn't done anything wrong (or so I thought.) I had to suffer the feelings of rejection and a low self image… and I had been faithful. I was the one who wasn't on the phone making calls to our ministry leaders and checking in on their well being and the progress of the marriage classes like I had done before. I had built so many close friendships with those calls. Why did I have to pay the price of someone else's disobedience? Why did I have to face the shame of walking out the discipline of a choice I hadn't made? It was a very unpleasant time for me. One morning as I prayed, God softly spoke to my heart.

"You keep saying 'Me, Me, Me, I, I, I.' When you married and entered into covenant with your husband, you became WE. There is no more 'I' and there is no more 'Me'. Whenever one of you sins, it brings consequences to both of you. Whenever one of you does well, it brings blessing to both of you."

"Wow! That really stinks when it's the consequence I'm reaping and not the blessing." I jokingly said to God, "I wish I'd considered that fact a little more before I said 'I do'."

We were out of the role of being worship leaders, and the ones who had taken over didn't have a lot of experience. The worship at church moved like a wagon traveling on square wheels. Then I started getting calls from the congregation members begging for just me to come back. They agreed that Glen needed a time of discipline, but they wanted the original team back, minus Glen, until he was ready. I felt pulled in my flesh to do it, but the Holy Spirit said "Stay." Here was the test of living in a state of "WE" rather than "ME."

As I relinquished my own desires and leaned on the truth of covenant, I began to see clearly that those who were calling me and asking me to come back were in disobedience. They were ignoring the authority set in place through the decision of the pastor and were seeking control in a situation that was uncomfortable for them. We all had things to learn. It was difficult to see the church members struggle. We knew that it was the effects of sin that came from our household. Now they, too, were paying a price. Forgiveness is freely given by God, but the effects of sin are still very real and painful. We learned that even our own church had to suffer for a while because of the disobedience.

Now was the time to rebuild in our own home and clean out the wrong that was causing so much pain. Frankly though, I didn't want to focus on our marriage. We had been giving out to others, but there were areas in our own lives that didn't line up with what we were teaching. We had learned how to work around them and ignore the problem.

For years I had allowed Glen to speak to me in a derogatory way. I had taken on the role of a doormat. When he hurt me with his words, I would go in another room, so he wouldn't see me cry. I was always quick to say "I'm sorry" just to avoid getting into an argument; and I said it even when I didn't feel I'd done anything wrong. I had developed the attitude that no matter what I did, it wouldn't be good enough, so during the day I did whatever I wanted. Just before Glen would come home from work, I would get nervous about the things left undone and I would rush around trying to clean everything up to avoid a conflict. I dreaded conflict, so if Glen ever wanted to talk out an issue, I would avoid it if we didn't agree.

I had developed my own habit of deception whenever I thought Glen would get mad about something. If he asked why something wasn't done, or why the kids had done something wrong, I would lie to cover up the truth just to avoid a confrontation. Sometimes I would have to make a list in my mind of the lies, so I wouldn't accidentally expose my own pattern of deception.

When we were left to face each other without any responsibilities for other people we were a sad sight.

I started to become focused on myself again and angry enough that I wasn't going to take any more of what I now labeled as abuse. Feelings of justification for my own lack of discipline in our marriage crept in. I had allowed self-pity into my own heart as I accepted the role of a martyr.

The first argument we had after the revelation of adultery caused me to be angry instead of feeling like the victim. I couldn't believe that Glen had the nerve to accuse me of anything after what he'd done. His responses in the heat of the disagreement looked incredibly childish, and I was disgusted by even his facial expressions. How dare he dish out anything but respect to me, after I had gone amazingly out of my way to forgive his gigantic crime? I took off out of the house, which was a first for me, and walked to a field a few blocks away. Plopping down in the dirt, I began to plead my case to God. As you can probably guess, it wasn't long before the Holy Spirit showed me the mountain of pride I had allowed myself to build. My choice to forgive didn't give me a badge that exempted me from being wrong. I had let myself believe that I was the good spouse' and Glen was the unworthy subject. Oh goodie! It was time to repent again. I went home and apologized for my part in the argument.

Within weeks of sharing this situation with our church I was faced with another temptation. A former boyfriend from Jr. High and High school called me after hearing of our struggle. He told me everything I wanted to hear. He said I had always been beautiful to him, and Glen didn't know the treasure he was holding. I let the conversation continue and remembered how sweet he was. I reminisced with him about some of the childhood memories we shared. He told me he had gone through betrayal in his own life, and he knew the pain of being the "victim" of adultery. My heart went out to him in understanding, and also in defense that such a sweet guy would have to go through the now familiar pain of betrayal. There was an instant connection of like-mindedness. For over 30 minutes I allowed myself to be fed by his words. I wanted so badly to hear that there wasn't anything wrong with me. I had felt so ugly and unwanted since Glen's confession, and my pride lapped up the affection and compliments like a thirsty dog in a desert.

I hadn't made Glen's requests a priority in our marriage up to that point. I would forget things that he would ask me to do. Sometimes I made mistakes out of being absent-minded and other times out of not giving him the respect he needed. I remember Glen asking me a couple of times, "Is there something wrong with you? Are you retarded or something?" They were words that cut deeply.

Now here I was being told that I was priceless, and that this former boyfriend had never stopped loving me. I still had feelings for him as well; he was my first boyfriend. We began to share some memories of fun things we had done with the youth group at our church when we were kids. I felt that familiar bond of friendship with him. He finally asked me if I would like to meet him for lunch sometime, and that's what shocked me back into reality. I quickly prayed silently in my mind for forgiveness, and asked God for wisdom. I told him, "If either of us wants to have a successful marriage, we need to not see or talk to each other, and we each need to focus on our own spouse."

It was hard. I felt like I was cutting short a good massage. I didn't want to reject him, when I felt like he had given me a glass of water in a desert of thirst; but I hung up and immediately called Glen and told him what had happened. I knew if I dwelt on it too long, it would lead down a dangerous path. Glen was understanding, and surprisingly not angry.

After the phone call, I could see how my state of selfish thinking had put me in a vulnerable place. I had set myself up for an attack, and the enemy had accepted my invitation. This temptation had looked so good, and felt so good; I understood how easy it would have been for Glen to fall.

I began to wonder if he had felt a lack of love too. I looked at the way I spoke to him, touched him, spoke of him to others, served him out of love and gave him preference. I found I was lacking. Since I had been a Christian longer than Glen, I took on the role of the spiritual leader. Anything he said, I weighed against my own "superior" knowledge. I gave him no respect, except to give in when I was afraid of his temper.

The Lord showed me that Glen needed to learn unconditional love and acceptance. He only allowed himself to receive love on a performance basis. His tendency towards perfection caused him to accept love, only if he thought he deserved it. He didn't know how to be nurtured.

God was showing me the root of the problem.

Glen has served in the military since years before we were married. With that length of service, he has moved up, considerably, in rank. He has the respect of those serving underneath his authority. When he is working on the base, he is given honor by those who see his rank and understand what it takes to earn his position. When he was at home, before God showed me my sin of disrespect, he had no recognition for his authority. At work he was honored, at home he was dishonored. Which people do you suppose he wanted to be around?

I asked God to begin showing me how to express honor and love to Glen in a way that he could receive it. I wanted him to know that I was offering love on an unconditional basis. If he never performed well again in any situation, I would still love and respect him. I repented for focusing only on my own needs and prayed for an understanding heart towards my husband.

It took effort on my part as I learned to praise him for the little things. Sometimes I wondered if I was sending the wrong message by suddenly complimenting his efforts so soon after his confession of unfaithfulness. I found it hard to find things to compliment.

I remember my dad teaching me to say something nice, even if the only thing I could find to say was that I liked the way he tied his shoes. The harder it was to find something, the harder I had to look; and looking hard was the key to finding the hidden treasures within him.

I learned that Glen had an entire treasure chest full of jewels. All I had to do was show Glen that I recognized his gifts, and he gladly brought them out for viewing. My mentality went from thinking that it was God and me against Glen, to realizing that God loved both of us the same. He wanted to see us both well and whole and functioning in the wonderful creativity He had given us. How selfish I had been to look at Glen's faults and refuse to draw out his talents, so I could appear more righteous than he. I decided to be a treasure hunter from now on. After all, Glen is God's creation, and therefore, the treasure is endless.

A TOUGH LESSON

Our state directors, who had kept in close contact, paid for a plane ticket to fly us to a neighboring state to stay with a couple who had experience in adultery recovery. They had walked through adultery healing years before. We had many questions, even though we knew we were making progress.

Our time with them was precious, as they welcomed us into their home for a few days. They encouraged us to read the Bible together and to pray as a couple every day.

We sat in their living room and shared our similar stories. They had such a love and trust between them that was incredible to watch.

As they interacted with one another, I noticed that there was no trace of hurt, from the adultery, left between them. They were very much in love, and radiated an immense amount of joy. What blessed me was that even though they talked about their painful past, there was nothing left there still causing pain. It gave me hope that total recovery was indeed possible.

On the second day, during our morning devotions, I shared with them some of the things I was still struggling with. They listened along with Glen, and when I finished dumping on them, the husband asked Glen to tell me he was sorry. Glen said he'd already done that, several times. The husband insisted he tell me again that he was sorry for the pain he had caused me. Glen, getting a little frustrated, asked: "How many times do I have to say I'm sorry for the same thing? Do I have to pay penance for the rest of my life?" he sincerely wanted to know how long this would take.

"You have to say it as many times as SHE needs it. You have to say it when you even think she may need to hear it," he answered.

"But if I've already said it, why do I need to repeat it over and over? She heard me the first time."

"That's what she needs to hear. That is what it is going to take for her to know you truly are sorry. It doesn't matter if you have already apologized. If she needs you to do it again, do it again, and mean it. It is a step you can do to help her with the healing she is going through."

Glen's voice began to raise a little as the two of them struggled over the issue. Apologizing had never come easily for Glen. As they argued it out, I heard God's gentle voice remind me again that love, for Glen, was received on a performance basis. To admit he was wrong was to admit, in his own mind, that he was unworthy.

That "discussion" was one of the hardest things for me to sit through. There I was, a woman who hates confrontation, listening to these two men battle it out over something I needed. I just wanted to say, "Forget it! If you don't mean it, I don't want to hear it." But I kept silent (at least on the outside.)

I don't remember how long the two of them contended together, but it seemed like hours. In the end, God won. Glen had needed someone to contend with him, and this man had stepped up to the plate. I know it wasn't enjoyable for either of them, but Glen's heart changed toward me that day. I felt like I went home with a different man. Glen saw the need in me, to hear and know that he was truly sorry, as greater than his own need to be right. He became willing to "man up" to his responsibility and take the brunt of the blame, even though it hurt him to do so.

Whenever I began tossing any small fact around in my head about the affair and would ask Glen about it, he would say that he was sorry he had put me through what I was dealing with; and yes, it was genuine. I know he didn't always feel like it, but the fact that he was making an effort spoke volumes to me. His perspective since that day has been, "If that's what it takes to walk in healing, it's a pretty small thing to neglect doing."

There is something that strikes a chord of joy in me when I see the new tenderness God has given Glen. His willingness to develop a new pattern that is foreign to him, just so I can be more comfortable, is amazing to me. Seeing his attitude of self-sacrifice makes me more willing to give up my own habits of self-preservation. A new attitude of giving was planted that weekend in our home from that precious godly couple. Those saints were more instrumental in our healing than they will ever know this side of heaven.

NOT TAKING ADVANTAGE

I had to be careful not to take advantage of Glen's new willingness to apologize. I began to learn that there are times to bring things up, and times to just pray and ask God to help me through painful memories. If I had brought up accusations every time they popped into my head those first few months, we would have been accusing and apologizing every two minutes.

The trauma of having someone else's presence (the other woman) involved in our marriage caused an overpowering obsession in my mind for several months. Knowing that another woman had shared not only Glen's body, but also his heart, emotions and mind was too much to fathom. I felt constant pain those first few weeks.

After a while I began to think of other things, instead of the all-consuming cloud hanging over me. Slowly the trauma became something I had to forgive only every hour or two. Then there were several hours between praying through forgiveness. I remember feeling a huge milestone had been reached when I went to bed one night and realized that I hadn't thought about it all day long. That was quite a while down the road, but it did eventually come.

Forgiveness wasn't a one time act for me; any more than apologizing was a one time act for Glen. It was a constant attitude that required active participation on both of our parts. Learning to take every thought captive wasn't a natural response; it was a decided action, a decision that had to be made on a constant basis. Some days I did great; other days I didn't do so great.

It was a struggle for me not to develop the attitude of vindictiveness. When Glen did something wrong, I couldn't hold the adultery up in his face. When I did something wrong, I couldn't use the excuse, "Well at least I didn't do something as big as cheating on you!" Those thoughts were definitely there. The temptation to bring accusation was a constant irritation like an ugly wart on the bottom of a tender foot.

I've talked to many women over the years and listened to them replay their husbands' sins, trying to rehearse every tiny detail, fearing they may have missed something. The temptation is great to continue to drum up the feelings of hurt in our lives. It would be so easy to ask every question about Glen's affair that pops in my head; but in the long run, I would be torturing myself as well as him. I would be trying to keep alive a tragedy that is long over. What is the advantage of that? To nurse and rehearse the same offense for years down the road, is the same as tying a corpse to my body, hoping to get away from the smell of death. The only way to breathe fresh air is to untie the dead body, and let it go.

Yes, Glen is willing to apologize for every offense he's done against me. My responsibility is to determine my "need" from my "want." I can't take advantage of a good thing and turn it into a pit of destruction. I have to be wise in when to keep my mouth closed.

The tremendous help was that we spent a great deal of time talking. The man I was forgiving wasn't a memory. We had stayed together with determination to work things out in spite of the pain. I forced myself to lie beside him in our bed to go to sleep at night, because I refused to let the enemy tell him he was an outcast, or tell me I was better than him. I was forgiving the one I was building a new relationship with.

We learned each other's feelings on things we had done for years out of everyday habit. We prayed a lot. And as we began to knit together a closer relationship out of our unraveled marriage, it began to take on a different look. God wasn't just restoring what we had been before; He was redeeming us to the one flesh relationship He had designed with Adam and Eve. I believe it was the first time in our marriage that we honestly knew the other's heart.

I know there was a new attitude formed in Glen's heart. Because several years later, when Glen and I were driving down the road, out of the blue I told him, "Sometimes when we are driving through our city and pass a motel, I wonder if that is one of the places you and the other woman have been in together." (It's something that had bothered me off and on for a long time.) I had no idea what his response was going to be. Would he give me names of places? Yes, I know he would if I asked. He blessed me so much more though, when he reached over and took my hand. "I'm sorry, Honey." He spoke so gently and with heartfelt love, that my question was answered just knowing that he genuinely cared and truly was sorry.

It's a level of tenderness that we never had before. I can trust Glen to own up to his mistakes when he needs to, and he can trust me that I will not dwell on those mistakes.

Sometimes when I look back, I think the breaking that took place when we walked out discipline was very necessary. Glen didn't "get away" with his sin. There were consequences; but those consequences led to repentance. We were both broken, but thankfully God never deems anyone unfixable. It's not that God planned it, but through the cracks in our broken hearts, He poured out his love more than ever before. I believe we are more able to demonstrate His love because those cracks are there. When we minister to couples now, there is a deeper understanding of their pain and an empathy that we never had while ministering in the past.

God knew that we needed tenderness between us, and He knew how to supply it.

Philippians 4:19 ". . . my God shall supply all your needs according to His riches in glory in Christ Jesus." (NAS)

That's a pretty abundant supply to draw from; way more than any of our needs could ever require.

RETURNING TO INTIMACY

One of the questions I had, but was afraid to ask anyone, was; "How long will it take before we are able to be intimate again?" I finally found an article someone had copied for me that said simply, "...not as long as you might think." I pieced that together with other bits of information from books and magazines that said things like, "Take the time necessary to minister to each other." and "Go slowly back into physical touch." One article told the offending spouse to wait patiently, even stopping in the middle of love making, if the other needed to back away. I was so thankful for those wise words. I had no idea of what was an acceptable timeframe. This wasn't something I could look up in scripture. No where in Leviticus does it say "Thou shall lie with thy husband 30 days after he repents of adultery." There was no key or timeframe mentioned. I could only find passages on stoning. The laws concerning unfaithfulness were established before the crucifixion, before forgiveness was made available through the blood of Jesus. There wasn't a set time to return to intimacy because in the time the laws were laid out, the adulterer was stoned to death. Returning to love making wasn't an issue.

Intimacy came more quickly than I had thought, though. God was moving in our hearts so fast, that as we experienced a stronger tie in the spirit and soul realms, a physical response naturally followed. I almost felt guilty that it was just a few short weeks, because I had figured it would be months. There was a time or two in the beginning that I had to stop because the feelings of hurt flooded back in unexpectedly. I wondered when Glen touched me, if he had touched "her" the same way. If he wanted to try something new, I had to fight thoughts and wonderings if it was because he had done that with her. Mental images of him in an embrace or sexual act with someone else would cause immediate nausea.

My emotional battle, with knowing my body wasn't as sexually appealing as hers, tried to plague me as I imagined her flat tummy and fuller breasts. I had to fight hard to focus on the good. It was a war in my head that seemed to kick decisive forgiveness against anger and pain. I remember saying to myself over and over "My marriage! My husband! Focus on the two of us, nothing more!"

Glen was very patient with me, and I never felt judged by him when I would have to back up and wrestle things out in my mind. Sometimes scripture would even pop into my head that came from my fleshly desire to strike back. Things like, "If your hand offends you cut it off……….." from Matthew 5:30 (I might add that we had raised horses, calves and goats when I was growing up. I worked for a veterinarian for a couple of years, so I knew how certain procedures were done; and I even had on our shelf, the tools needed to perform the procedure.) I know, I know, it was Scripture out of context, but I did have vindictive thoughts once in a while. I knew my flesh was responding to offense. I had chosen to let go of offense. I had lain down my hurt and chosen God's healing. Picking it up again after so much progress would be foolish and destructive. The Holy Spirit gently reminded me that every second I allowed vindictive thoughts to entertain me; I was squelching His counsel and quenching His Spirit from ministering to our need.

Praying together before intimacy helped more than anything. Just as in the first few minutes after Glen's confession, when the Holy Spirit directed me step by step, I found His leading in the return to physical touch. There were specific steps God had me take in the area of physical affection to demonstrate a heart of forgiveness. Rather than risk the chance of being too graphic, I will suffice it to say that God orchestrated step by step the answer to every question I took to Him in prayer. He was direct as to what I should do to hurdle the blocks that the wounding had caused. God's detail in the physical realm was a reminder to me that sexual acts between husband and wife were His idea. He created it. He wasn't embarrassed by my graphic questions; and He wasn't embarrassed to answer in specific ways.

Glen recognized at different times that the Lord was leading me in different physical expressions, and we were both grateful for His detailed counsel to us.

All of our married life I had thought of sex as a physical act that was done out of a loving response. I knew that God had intended it to be a place of healing, but I had envisioned that to be healing from small arguments and harsh words.

Obviously, there has to be a certain amount of forgiveness operating in order for both parties to consent to physical closeness. That had been so true up to that point in our marriage; but as God began to do His deep work in our lives, I began to truly understand why God created physical intimacy.

Our obedience in forgiveness, praying together, reading the Scriptures, talking out suspicions and planning ahead for the vision God was imparting in our hearts brought us together in a powerful closeness that was totally new. I went from wondering in the beginning how I would ever be able to let Glen touch me again, to a natural response of desiring his touch. We each felt so close in the spirit and heart (soul) that responding physically was just an outward expression of the new closeness we felt. God was birthing an entirely new meaning of sex in our hearts.

I could sense the warfare taking place as the devil lost his foothold in our marriage. The years of pornographic influence and worldly views took on an obviously cheapened look. How do you compare anything to the joy of being in God's presence together and reveling in His Glory?

Never again will we say to God like we had before; "You'd better leave the bedroom now. This is going to get ugly." It is as if we would shut the door on Him out of our discomfort in His presence. Isn't that just what Adam and Eve did when they sewed fig leaves to cover themselves? It was shameful for us in the past, because there was hidden sin. Now that the dirt of iniquity had been washed off of us by the precious blood of Jesus, there was no more shame. We were able to gladly invite God in to our room as we opened His wedding gift to us, and then to thank Him for the joy the gift created. There truly is nothing in a marriage bed more awesome than being in the presence of Jesus in complete purity. It is not a carnal act because it was God's creation in the first place. Mankind's own interpretation and the influence of the enemy is what distorted our view. Sex is spiritual warfare and, "…The weapons of our warfare are not carnal, but mighty through God to the pulling down of strongholds." (2 Corinthians 10: 4 KJV) What a joy it has been to have the strongholds in our lives pulled down by this precious time together.

When God heals, places of wounding become stronger than they were before.

THE "OCTOPUS" OF WOUNDING

I have found that just as an octopus has many legs, so do some deep hurts. We may conquer an issue such as intimacy or honesty when recovering from adultery, only to find that another issue waits in the shadows for us to arrive. Little did I know that a "leg" of distrust from the "octopus of wounding" could strike from out of the shadows.

After about six months of walking out healing, I woke up at 4:00 in the morning to find Glen gone from our bed. I was concerned that he was sick, so I went to the bathroom and checked. He wasn't there. I looked all over the house and couldn't find him. I looked out the windows and couldn't see him outside either.

Our car was home, but the front door of our house was unlocked. I had an instant fear that "the woman" had come and picked him up. It was the only logical solution. They hadn't spoken for a long time, and I thought they must have called to check up on each other, and things had gotten out of hand again. It was still dark, and I just knew that the two of them were together again. The thought made me sick.

The familiar feeling of nausea and shakes began to creep over me, and I sank to the couch in defeat. I started to pray that the Lord would help me know what to do if they drove up, and she dropped him off. I wondered to myself if I would have the strength to do it all over again. I thought that I had probably let him off too easily before. He didn't know how much pain it had really caused me, because I had chosen to forgive him so quickly.

I was in the process of deciding what I should do, when God clearly reminded me that Satan is the accuser of the brethren (Rev. 12:10) and Jesus is the intercessor (Rom. 8:34.) "You are siding with the accuser. Come over to my side. Pray, instead of jumping to conclusions." I began to pray, and as I did, my mind quieted down and I settled into peace. When I finally allowed my imagination to come back to reality, I began to hear a scraping sound coming from outside. I went out to investigate, and found Glen by the side of the house shoveling weeds.

"What in the world are you doing out here at four o'clock in the morning?" I asked, thinking that "she" must have dropped him off already, and this was his cover up.

"It's nice and cool out here, I couldn't sleep, and this weeding needs to be done." He replied.

I looked around and realized that there was a large amount of work done. Glen had been out there a long time…the whole time.

I could have screamed (out of joy, relief, frustration with myself or him; take your pick) but I had definitely been put to shame for my quick jump to judgment.

I went back into the house, and again heard the voice of the ultimate Counselor. "It's not a sin to assume someone is innocent, only to learn that they have betrayed you. It IS a sin, to assume someone is guilty, when they are, in fact, innocent." I repented.

It was a huge lesson for me. Every time I wonder if there is something going on with Glen that I should know about, I remember that morning and those clear words from the Holy Spirit.

I don't ever want to side with the accuser. I hope Glen will always assume the best of me, and I must be willing to offer him the same respect.

There seemed to be many ugly things attached to adultery recovery. It was like each octopus leg caused its own set of damage.

Obviously, trust was an area where destruction had hit. Learning to put my hope and confidence in Jesus, instead of my husband, helped me put in perspective who really was my source. Jesus, the One who was and is ultimately trustworthy, is a completely faithful foundation that I know I can trust.

Another leg caused a blow to my self-esteem. I obviously had to deal with feelings of inadequate looks. I'm definitely not a qualifier for magazine covers. My friend's daughter was going through betrayal in her marriage. When my friend talked to me about it, she said "...but my daughter is beautiful, I don't understand." There is some huge misconception, that many women have, that makes us think outward beauty gives us power. The way our world works, there is some truth in that; but we cannot believe that it offers us immunity from betrayal. At one point I dyed my hair a bleach blonde trying to make myself more attractive. I went without eating for several weeks both out of trauma and out of a will to make myself thinner. It only caused me to gain more weight in the end, when I was so weak that I had to start eating again. I know that even the most beautiful women still face adultery, but there is a temptation to believe that if I were more beautiful, he wouldn't have to look somewhere else. The truth is that it isn't a beauty issue, it's a heart issue. I have to remind myself to keep my perspective. This was an outward response to a spiritual issue.

Still another appendage of that relationship that I learned about, at a doctor's visit years later, was a sexually transmitted disease. I was instantly ashamed and angry that I was carrying a remnant of Glen's sin that left me feeling dirty and tainted. I felt victimized all over again. All the questions of "why" flooded through my mind as I battled with my attitude on the drive home. What I was really upset about was my pride. I didn't want my doctor to think I was a cheap, loose slut. I was beyond that. I didn't want to be classified with the sinners. Ha! What did I think I was? I may not have been guilty of the sin of adultery, but take your pick of hundreds of other sins. I was looking down on women in countless different situations and putting myself above them. What an ugly attitude of self-righteousness I had! Like my sins are any more pure than the next person's sin.

It boiled down to recognizing that although another repercussion of Glen's sin had manifested, the sin itself had not reoccurred. Instead of allowing myself to feel punished for my husband's act, I had to take hold of an attitude of humility for all the physical pain my own sin caused Jesus to endure on the cross. Not the least of them was self-righteousness. If he was willing to take all that on for me, I could certainly allow some grace toward my husband for this small inconvenience I now faced.

Distrust, self-esteem issues, self-righteousness, the octopus legs at times seemed endless. When I was fighting three or four "legs"; it seemed like I was fighting ten or twelve. Now, as each one is defeated, I gain a deeper trust in the healing power of the blood of Christ. I'm learning not to begrudge myself healing time when a defeated leg tries to raise up again. Any size of hurt requires time to heal.

When I had back surgery and tried to help my husband butcher his elk a week later, I became fully aware that I hadn't taken the time necessary to heal. When I tried to move a piano 4 days after giving birth, I suddenly remembered that softened tissue needs a chance to strengthen before strenuous work can resume.

In the same way that a physical incision needs to mend, a broken heart takes time too. I didn't need to put on a fake face of happiness, when I was feeling emotional pain, any more than I would need to lie about my ability to move furniture after giving birth.

It is alright to cry. It is alright to plead to God for help, because the weight of those "legs" is too great for me to carry on my own. My responsibility is to make sure that natural grieving doesn't give way to self-pity. Tears are a normal result of pain.

No matter how many "legs" or facets of damage need to be restored, God promises that He will give wisdom to all who ask. He is faithful to show us how to walk out of pain and into healing.

James 1:5 (KJV) says, "If any of you lack wisdom, let him ask of God, that giveth to all men liberally, and upbraideth not; and it shall be given him."

WISDOM IN KNOWING WHEN TO SHARE

There is a delicate balance between putting on a mask and pretending that everything is fine, and blubbering out my hurt and anger to anyone who will listen. My mom taught me that before speaking to people about an issue it must pass through three doors. First, is it true? Second, is it kind? Third, is it necessary?

That's been a useful gauge in many conversations. Sometimes I find it necessary to talk things out; but I have to be careful to be kind. Something may be kind, but is it completely true? Have you ever heard someone say things that are true and kind, but the timing was off and it was really unnecessary? That's a difficult thing for those of us who get on a roll and really love to talk. As long as the three doors are passable, it's probably all right to share. If it isn't true, kind, and necessary, it probably doesn't need to be said. I love the saying "It's better to be silent and thought a fool, than to open your mouth and remove all doubt."

The other gauge my dad gave me was to ask myself, "Is this person part of the problem or part of the solution?" It's a great way to keep from back-biting others. It's also a great way to keep my attitude and my tongue bridled.

We all have different personalities and needs, but our basic make-up is the same. We need each other. That's why scripture tells us not to forsake the fellowship of the saints (Hebrews 10:25); to confess our sins to one another, and to pray for each other (James 5:16). When we went public with our situation, it was to the groups of people directly affected by it. We let ourselves be open and transparent for accountability and for healing. Sharing at the right moment, has given others in our lives, permission to be open to seek help, or share wisdom as well.

Now, as we minister to other couples in the same situation, it is a blessing to be part of what may be their solution. God never wastes a trial. We have learned a lot. We are still learning a lot. We haven't "arrived" by any means, but the beautiful change in our marriage is just too wonderful to keep to ourselves when we see those around us struggling through the same issues.

Yes, this is a terrible thing to happen to any couple, but we can testify that it doesn't have to be the final blow that ends a marriage. For us, making the choice to walk out healing was the best move we ever made together. It was redemption for not only our marriage, but also for our children, our families and our acquaintances. If we had chosen to end it all, our children would have learned the way of bitterness too. They would have been taught that some things are just too big to forgive, to conquer, or to get victory over. Instead they have learned that the same forgiveness that the Lord offers to us through His blood can be extended through his people.

Our children know what our struggles are, and what life is like on the other side of healing. They see the deep love that God has restored between us, and they know that we are fully committed to God, to each other, and to them. It's a security that can't be matched. They never have to ask us if we are going to get a divorce. If they hear a disagreement, they know it is temporary. Glen and I made a vow that we will never use the word "divorce" in our home pertaining to our marriage. Our children know that we will never make a decision to divorce; we made that promise to them. We believe every child deserves that kind of security. We believe every couple deserves the wonderful healing and complete oneness that is enjoyed when God is allowed to move.

My Grandpa Blackburn had a saying that he recited to me many times. It went like this: "What you do, do with all your might. Things done by halves are never done right." I love that saying. It is similar to Ecclesiastes 9:10. When my grandpa would repair fence, dig post holes, halter break a foal, churn ice-cream, or even rest, he would put his whole heart into it. He often said "Work hard, rest hard, play hard." It's a great motto.

As we forced our feet to tread the path of healing, it took a great amount of determination. It was hard work. We wanted the job to be done well, and not done by "half." Our marriage needed repair, but our children, and the legacy given to them, needed to be mended and reinforced as well. We prayed for timing, and watched for when our children were at an age where they could understand and be responsive to Glen's confession. Since we use our testimony to help other couples, there are many people who know our past. We don't want to overlook the protection of our children's hearts as we minister to others. We wanted them to hear it from us and not from someone else. We know God wants to do His awesome work in their lives too.

It was years down the road when Glen talked to our children. One-by-one as each reached the appropriate age, we set apart a time and talked with them as a couple. We were careful to demonstrate our one-flesh mindset, and our determination, that we are married for our lifetime. With the pain gone, and our love renewed, our children have been able to see for themselves how powerful repentance and forgiveness really is. To be honest, when we took them somewhere so we could talk to them privately, they were just relieved that they weren't in trouble. At first we thought that was because they didn't grasp the depth of what we were saying; but I have come to realize that they easily received the news because they were already living in observation of God's work in progress. They see the love between Glen and me on a daily basis. We have grumpy and stressed days, just like everyone else, but there are no underlying currents of resentment that they have to dodge. They don't live in fear of being swept into a river of hateful words.

It took courage for Glen to confess to our kids. I am grateful that his heart has remained repentant and soft. He has been careful to watch for our children's response to him. He has stayed humble, knowing that defending their spirits, rather than his actions, is the key to relationship with them. It was a step of faith each time we talked to them. We hoped with all our hearts that it would not damage their relationship with us.

Sometimes it's just plain scary to step out where there is no guarantee of safe ground. We knew that obedience in transparency to our children could cause problems. We also knew God was asking us to do it. Faith became the ground for us as we took the risk. I'm so grateful for forgiving children! They have been open to us, and have accepted Glen's apologies with amazing readiness. We are absolutely blessed.

Two of them, along with one of their friends, drew the pictures at the end of this book recapping points of emphasis. They captured the heart of our message so wonderfully.

Jesus is the author and finisher of our faith (Hebrews 12:2.) When we allow Him, the author, to write on our hearts the measure of faith needed to get through the healing process, he is able to finish His awesome work. I didn't have enough faith to get through this. Glen didn't have enough faith to get through this, but God knew without a doubt that we could. He authored what we needed when we gave Him permission. He could see past the rubble into our victory.

I can honestly say that I am grateful now for the journey. As crazy as that sounds, I am just so thankful that we are not what we used to be. I'm not grateful that the sin occurred, but the sin was an issue before it ever happened. It was something that occurred out of an already wounded marriage. If the whole thing never would have come to a head, forcing us to deal with the root cause, we might still be stuck in our rut. Choosing to heal from adultery was our turning point, our line in the sand.

It used to be, that when Glen touched me, I would feel dirty. I could actually see in the Spirit when he had an ugly demon of lust on his back. If he had been looking at pornographic material, I could sense it in his touch. It was so blatant at times that I would cringe and begin praying under my breath for God to take away the lust, so I could respond to my husband without feeding the unclean spirit hanging on him.

When Glen was forced to face the issue of adultery out in front of so many of our friends, it caused him to be repulsed by what had entrapped him. I remember him telling me, soon after his confessions to everyone that the thought of returning to his old patterns of lust made him sick to his stomach. That spirit of lust has been removed by Glen's repentance from sin. That doesn't mean that he doesn't have to deal with temptation anymore, but he now knows the freedom of walking in victory over the temptation. Now that we have walked out the discipline of the Lord, and been down the road of recovery, Glen says he feels as if he's been let out of prison.

What a superior job the Holy Spirit does! I tried for a long time to get Glen to feel that way, but everything I did seemed to backfire. When I allowed the Lord to do His own work without my interference, amazingly, Glen responded! So, yes, if adultery is what it took to break the cycle of lust, and public repentance is what it took to drive out that demon from our home, it was worth adultery to me.

So now do we just openly share with anyone? Surprisingly, yes, IF the Holy Spirit directs. We don't just blatantly blab to everyone, but we try to stay open to the Holy Spirit's direction whenever He tells us to share. I've never gone up to someone and introduced myself as a survivor of the big marriage catastrophe. We don't wear t-shirts announcing our history. God knows when our story will help encourage another couple; we just need to be willing to obey when He says to share.

I remember about a year before Glen let me know about the adultery, we had a missionary couple come and stay at our house for an evening. We were visiting about ministry and their lives in Mexico. Out of the blue, the husband pulled out a book someone had written on adultery. "This is a really good book, if you know anyone who is trying to recover from adultery, give this to them." Glen, still in the middle of covering things up quickly changed the subject; but I made a mental note to keep it in mind for referring to couples who might need it. That book later gave me an incredible amount of encouragement when I found that we were the couple who needed it. That man couldn't have known what was happening in our marriage. He was from another country. He was responding to the Holy Spirit's direction to tell us about the book. God knew I would need it, and He used that man to prepare me for what was coming.

We want to be that kind of vessel for someone else. It's not pleasant to drag out our dirty laundry, but I will say it again, God never wastes a trial. Part of the joy of healing is being able to show others that even if they are "road kill" on the highway of pain, God is the giver of life. He can breathe life into a dead and decaying marriage. We've seen it over and over again. The only dead marriage is the marriage where one or both partners refuses God's restoration, and willfully decides to walk away from fighting for their home. When both spouses are willing to let God work in their marriage, nothing can tear them apart.

CREATING A GOOD HABIT

My dad preached a sermon once that centered on creating good habits to replace bad ones. He talked of how it takes twenty-one days to make something a habit. If we do something every day for twenty–one days straight, it begins to become a part of our every day lives.

I was thinking on that sermon when God showed me that part of the answer to my reoccurring feelings of hurt was to make forgiving a new habit.

He had me write down a list of verses on forgiveness and place Glen's and my names in them to make them personal. Then He had me read over them every day, out loud, to different friends to whom I was accountable or who were also struggling with forgiveness.

I shared these with over twenty-one people over the next three weeks, they are powerful.

As I read them out loud over and over, I believe they were written on the tablets of my heart. These verses have changed my life.

They are based on the following Scriptures, but in a loose enough translation that I could apply them personally. If you want an exact translation, I encourage you to look up the references.

I'd like to share them with you and ask that where you see our names, put in your own name and the name of someone you are choosing to forgive.

Here is the life changing list:

> Matthew 6:14-25 If I forgive Glen when he sins against me, my Heavenly Father will also forgive me. But if I do not forgive Glen when he hurts me, my Father will not forgive me when I hurt Him.
>
> Luke 23:34 Jesus said, "Father forgive them, for they do not know what they are doing." WHILE they were crucifying Him.
>
> Matthew 5:23-24 If I come before God and remember that something that I have caused is still bothering Glen, I will stop offering praise offerings or service to God and go quickly to Glen, apologize to him, be reconciled, and then come back and offer my sacrifice to God.
>
> Mark 11:25 If I am praying, and find I still hold unforgiveness towards Glen, or anyone else, I will first forgive him so that my Father will forgive me.
>
> Proverbs 17:9 When I cover Glen's sin and quit nagging about his mistakes, I promote Love; but if I repeat the matter, it will separate us.
>
> Acts 7:60 Stephen said, "Lord do not hold this sin against them." WHILE they were stoning him.
>
> Romans 2:4-5 Laura, remember how patient God is being with you, and don't forget to appreciate it. Can't you see that He has been waiting all this time without punishing you to give you time to return from your sin of unforgiveness towards Glen? His kindness is meant to lead you to repentance. If I don't listen and hold unforgiveness, I will be saving up terrible punishment for myself because of my stubbornness, for the day of wrath will come when God will judge the world.
>
> 1 Corinthians 13:5 I will not be rude to Glen, or be looking at my hurts in a selfish way. I will not get angry at him easily, and I will not keep a record of how many times he has hurt me, or done something wrong.

1 Peter 4:8 Above all, I will love Glen deeply, because love makes up for a multitude of faults.

Isaiah 43:25 I will do as God does and not think of Glen's sin any more.

Psalm 103:12 I will not hold on to the hurt Glen has caused me, and I will do what it takes to remove my unforgiveness towards him; as far from me as the east is from the west.

Psalm 103:2-4 Yes, I will bless the Lord and not forget the glorious things He does for me. He forgives all my sins and heals me. He ransoms me from Hell and surrounds me with loving kindness and tender mercies.

Matthew 7:15 If I don't criticize Glen, he won't criticize me. He will treat me the same way that I treat him. I can't very well help Glen with what I think he should fix if my own faults are so large that I can't see around them. First I must make sure my own heart is clean, so that I will be able to see how I should PRAY for Glen.

Luke 6:37 I must never criticize Glen or it will all come back on me, and I will be criticized. If I go easy on him, he will go easy on me.

Luke 7:47 My sins, even though they are many, have been forgiven because I love Jesus so much. And it is because I have been forgiven so much, that I can love and forgive Glen in return.

1 John 2:4 I may say that I am going to Heaven because I am a Christian. But if I don't do what Jesus tells me to do, I am a liar.

1 John 3:4 If I hold on to my unforgiveness, I am against God because every sin is done against the will of God, including unforgiveness.

Proverbs 28:13 If I hide my unforgiveness or bury it, I will be unsuccessful, but if I confess and renounce it, I WILL find mercy.

Hebrews 12:15 I don't want to miss the grace of God by allowing a root of bitterness to grow up, cause trouble, and defile Glen and me.

Proverbs 26:17 Yanking a dog by the ears would be no more foolish than harboring unforgiveness for, or sticking my nose into business that does not concern me.

> Matthew 22:39 I must love Glen as much as I love myself.
>
> Matthew 5:44 I will love Glen even when I feel like we are enemies, and I will pray for him, even if he persecutes me.

And my favorite:

> Ephesians 2:14-16 Christ himself is our way of peace. He will make us a close and united couple and family. He will break down the wall of contempt that used to separate us. By His death, he ended the angry resentment between Glen and me. He took us, who were opposed to each other, and made us parts of Himself. He fused us together to become one new person, and at last there is peace. As parts of the same body, our anger towards each other has disappeared, for both of us have been reconciled to God. And so our feuds have ended at last at the cross.

I encourage you to copy these down for yourself and your spouse. Put your names in where they fit, and read them every day for three weeks or longer. Let them penetrate into your soul and spirit. Both you and your spouse, if possible, do this each day. If your spouse is not willing, do it as an act of faith and of obedience. Even if your spouse never wants to reconcile, you still need to be healthy and whole. Your heart needs to be right before God. He wants to dress and heal your wounds, but he won't do that if you refuse to allow him to. Let God reveal His way of healing. You'll have such sweet communion with Him as you spend time yielding to the softening of your heart.

Reading these aloud both confirmed them to my spirit and sealed them to my will. The other advantage I noticed was that the Lord had me call and speak these Scriptures to close friends who had picked up the offense against Glen. As they saw my active decision to walk in forgiveness, they too were able to release forgiveness towards him. God's word is truly quick, it is truly powerful, and it divided my decision, to allow healing, away from my desire for revenge. As the scriptures were read, they imbedded into my soul causing me to cling to God. The more I hung on to Him for life, the more I began to lose sight of my wounds.

The world tells us in so many different ways how we should take ownership of our hurts. We buy off on the idea that we will never be made whole again and we must learn to function in spite of the horrible scars. Some psychologists say we should embrace the wounding and make it a part of who we are. Contrast that to Jesus, who, after His death on the cross, says to us in Matthew 11:28 (KJV), "Come unto me all ye that labor and are heavy laden, and I will give you rest." What a difference to give ownership of our hurts to the one who paid the price for them, making it possible to melt them away. Yes, they can really dissipate and become a steppingstone of victory rather than a cornerstone of pain in the person I am. Offense then becomes an opportunity to see the miracle of redemption and restoration; but the choice is ours. Will we allow the sin of another to dictate who we are, or will we grasp onto the new identity that Jesus provided: health, hope, and life?

I don't want to be made up of a series of hurts. I want to be made up of a series of miracles; a picture of mercy, and a reflection of Christ.

UNDERSTANDING PAIN FROM ANOTHER ANGLE

Suppose Glen came home from the doctor's office and told me he had been diagnosed with an aggressive form of cancer. Let's also suppose that it is a type of cancer that is sometimes preventable, such as lung or liver cancer. How strange would it be if my initial response was, "How could you do this to ME!?" That would be an extremely selfish response to his diagnosis. But, how far away from that example is our same response to the sin of adultery. When Glen found himself trapped against a wall, separated by sin from his Savior, without seeing a way out, and headed straight for death, he was on his way to ruin just as much as if he were dying from a dreaded disease. Yes, it was his choice, and yes, he had repeatedly dipped into the poison of sin; but the poison none the less was coursing through his spiritual veins. His heart was hardening, and his life and joy were ebbing away.

When sin is repeated, our response to people around us becomes protected. We become so consumed with protecting our secret that we can no longer open up completely to those around us, especially those operating in the Holy Spirit and walking in discernment. We do the same thing when we are in pain physically. Our focus becomes turned inward and interruptions make us lose the focus necessary to deal with the intensity of the pain. Look at a woman in labor. When Glen would try to comfort me during early labor it was helpful, but as I moved into transition, his efforts to offer comfort were met with resistance and sometimes, quite frankly, with malice. Then when he tried to remind me how to breathe correctly, I would envision ripping his ears off.

During the three years that Glen was hiding his other relationship; I would drag him to numerous marriage and Christian events. I didn't know what our marriage problem was, but I knew we had some issue somewhere, because I felt a block in our transparency towards each other. I couldn't understand why he would snap at people sometimes in the middle of a conversation, causing them to back away. When people tried to get close, he would put up a wall. It was the same as seeing the symptom of cancer, knowing that there was a sickness of some sort, without identifying the cause. Since I couldn't see it, I just assumed he was being a "jerk." After the revelation of adultery and confession to others, I saw a new Glen. He was friendly in a group, his guard was let down, and he began to laugh and smile again. He no longer needed to protect himself by keeping people away who live and operate in the spiritual gift of discernment. He became free to be himself, without fear of exposing his hidden sin. People were no longer a threat; they became friends and fellow believers.

When I finally discovered what was happening, God showed me that although it was our marriage that was impacted, the sin (or cancer) was growing inside of Glen's heart. He was the one in serious trouble. His relationship with God had been jeopardized. That was scary! I knew that any marriage could be saved through the sheer will of two spouses, but, this was way more serious than even a marriage. This was eternal. It was as if Glen were walking towards a spiritual cliff and about to drop off the edge to his death. With that revelation, I suddenly turned my attention away from my own pain and felt an insatiable urge to reach out to prevent him from falling. What terrible pain he must have been in, to be in the place he was. What self-absorbing guilt must have been crushing his heart; and yet he had a desire to repent and see our marriage healed. He wanted to see me made whole again. It is the perfect glimpse of the tender heart that God was creating in him.

Pointing fingers at Glen for bringing adultery into our lives would be the same as pointing fingers at him if he were to be diagnosed with a deadly disease. Yes, sinning was a conscious choice, the same as if he were to smoke or drink, bringing on lung or liver cancer; but a selfish attitude focusing only on my own pain would ignore the need for him to be made well, not only of the sin, but of the horrible result from it.

Glen's choice to be vulnerable and obedient to God, and the Christian leadership over us eventually resulted in a pure heart. It was the "chemo" if you will, that destroyed the disease and root cause of sin. He had to humble himself and admit to everything, and then trust God to do the cleaning. He couldn't clean himself up, and then come to God. That would be like taking a muddy bath in order to be able to take a shower. He just simply yielded to God and decisively chose to put our marriage as a priority.

Each new revelation from the Holy Spirit has brought us a little closer to healing. During our walk through the "cleaning out" process, this revelation gave me strength. Relating adultery to cancer gave me the urgency to continue the healing process even when my emotions wanted to break for a pity party. If I were the only one to be healed, our marriage still would have been unhealthy.

There's healing for me when Glen is made whole. There is healing for Glen when I am made whole. There is healing for our children when their Dad and Mom are made whole.

There is healing for the Body of Christ when God's people are made whole and testify of His goodness. There is healing and hope for the world when they see a difference in our lives. They will know we are Christians by our love.

RETURNING TO MINISTRY

When our five month sabbatical from ministry at our church was over, we returned with a bit of hesitancy as well as excitement. We had come far in five months, and yet we felt stained in our own minds and unworthy to serve. We had experienced God's forgiveness and were walking in a new powerful one-flesh relationship. We were also fully aware that as we stepped up to lead worship, there was a congregation of eyeballs looking at us who were fully aware of our inadequacy. I remember thinking to myself that we had no business standing on that platform in front of anyone. I quietly prayed under my breath "God, this is the most humbling place I've ever stood…."

I was waiting for a sympathetic response from Him when out of the blue He answered me, "What a wonderful place for you to be."

I had to smile. Isn't that just like God? We were totally dependent on Him……Right where we needed to be. There certainly wasn't any point in trying to make ourselves look good. Any possibility of that was blown out of the water. There was nowhere to go, but to grab God's hand and trust that He would cover us. My prayer then, and now, too, when we lead anything, is that people will be able to look past the messenger and hear the message.

The next humbling step was to take a marriage class from leaders who had been our marriage students in a class years before. In fact, three of our former students participated in that class. We began again at square one. What is covenant? What is one-flesh?

Part of me felt like a sixth grader demoted to kindergarten. Most of me felt extremely grateful that they would even allow us to set foot back into the ministry at any level. As we went through those classes that we had taught for years, I noticed how different they seemed. I was sure they had rewritten the material to fit our situation. Things that I had skimmed over before jumped to life. Glen and I found ourselves plunging into these Scriptures that applied not just to other classmates, but intimately to our own marriage.

When we finished the class we had a new understanding of each and every principle. We had a new desire to teach the principles and help other couples who were as desperate as we had been. Amazingly, we were released to train as leaders, and eventually to lead our own groups again. God allowed us to serve him in spite of knowing our most ugly times and the things we have had to walk out. He opened His arms to us and allowed us to continue with the call on our lives, even though He knows we have failed. We thank God with all of our hearts for giving us another chance.

I once asked God why He would allow a marriage like ours, which had such failure written on it, to minister to others. He quickly began to parade people from Scripture through my mind: Paul, who was a murderer, wrote part of the New Testament. Jonah, who abandoned the call and ran, out of fear, was later used to answer THAT SAME CALL and help bring Nineveh to repentance. Peter, who went as far as to deny Jesus Christ, was welcomed back by Jesus himself! (John 21:15-17) Jesus told him, "If you truly love me, 'feed my lambs'" and again, "Feed my sheep."

Do you suppose the writers of Scripture were transparent in sharing their own inadequacies because they knew imperfect people would follow after them? I believe it without a doubt. If the church allowed only sinless people to minister, there wouldn't be a person alive worthy of serving. Jesus was the only perfect person to ever walk the face of the earth. If we remove everyone who has committed adultery from ministry, how many would be left in the pulpit? Everyone who even looks at a woman with lust in his heart has already committed adultery, according to Matthew 5:28. I'm so glad for the blood of Jesus. That blood, which washes us as white as snow, removes all of the stain of sin, sets us free to fulfill our call, and even better, allows us to have relationship with God himself!

God, in His wisdom, placed in each of His children the beautiful desire to help others. From this longing, stems a fantastic jewel of purpose. I remember a thought crossing my mind as I was praying through a difficult moment of our recovery. "Someday, you will be able to help others walk this difficult path. Since you have already come this way, you will be able to hand them a road map. When you find yourselves on the other side of this, don't forget to pass along the landmarks. In doing so, others will be spared wrong turns and lengthy agony."

I believe that thought was from God. He knew we needed a strong sense of meaning. It gave a bit of purpose to what we had dealt with. Every testimony begins with a test. Why waste the experience by succumbing to shame? This time in our lives was huge! It would be a waste to shove it in the closet and hope no one would ever find out. Besides, God has an amazing ability to turn what the Devil meant for destruction, into heavenly gain.

It was more like baby steps back into ministry, rather than a leap; but every little step felt like a leap in itself. Stepping back into service was another form of forcing ourselves to receive God's forgiveness. We had learned how to extend forgiveness, we had learned how to walk out forgiveness, now was the time to receive and walk IN forgiveness.

We can't shoot ourselves in the foot by refusing this important step of receiving. Remember, idolatry is putting something else above God,..... including placing our inadequacy above His call.

If you are reading this and have not received the forgiveness of God, you should know that it is simply a matter of asking. The payment for sin was already accomplished when Jesus died on the cross. He says, ". . . if you confess with your mouth Jesus as Lord, and believe in your heart that God raised Him from the dead, you shall be saved, for with the heart man believes, resulting in righteousness, and with the mouth he confesses, resulting in salvation." (Romans 10:9-10 NAS)

I cannot imagine trying to go through life without the wonderful Counselor I have in Jesus. He makes my life have meaning and purpose. He fills the void in the core of my being with His Holy Spirit, and showers me with love every day. He is faithful. He is faithful. He is faithful!

I pray that you will know the faithfulness and Grace of Jesus. Invite Him to take control of your life. He will never leave you alone. He will always love you…always and without fail.

If you are reading this and have disqualified yourself or allowed others to disqualify you from ministry, please know that God can still use you for His Glory. You are most likely better equipped now than you were before your trial.

Jesus' blood covers all. That means everything. If you have repented and are walking in healing, share your story. Ask God to show you today who needs to hear your testimony. Don't hoard it and hope others can find their own way through. Show someone, who needs to know, that victory is indeed available.

Allow God to minister through you. As long as you have breath, praise Him for His faithfulness. As long as you can speak, proclaim His goodness to all generations.

WHAT IF THERE IS NO REPENTANCE?

Unfortunately, some men and women have their sights set on continuing an adulterous relationship even after the sin has been discovered. Glen and I have talked to spouses on the receiving end of blatant sexual sin, and it is heartbreaking. Selfishness causes the offending member to be so absorbed in their lusts and desires that the marriage is tossed aside.

If you are the only one willing to work on your marriage right now, know that whether or not your spouse chooses to fix it, you still need to receive healing. Forgiveness does not hinge on your spouse being repentant. Forgiveness keeps YOUR heart right with God. He can restore and heal you much more quickly if he doesn't have to work around your bitterness. Your marriage is important to Him, and your own life is precious, so precious that He was willing to die for you. Keep your heart right before Him so that He can be your counselor.

Just as He guided me through every step, especially those horrible first few hours after Glen's confession, the Holy Spirit will guide you as well. His plans for you are greater than anything you could ever imagine. You have a purpose and an assignment. Whether your spouse remains in the marriage or not, there is a place for you in the arms of Jesus. Let Him comfort you and show you the depth of His devotion to you.

I had the advantage of a repentant husband by the time I learned what had happened. Many spouses don't get that luxury. There are times when it takes consequences for the guilty (Hebrews 12:4-11), and prayers and tears from the wronged, before repentance comes. Some repeat offenders need to be taught that their behavior will not be tolerated.

A time of separation is sometimes necessary. This is not a separation with the intent of divorce. This is a time for the offended to demonstrate that the repeated wounding will not be accepted any longer. Some nuts are tougher to crack, just as some spouses are harder to yield. If you do separate, make sure you stay willing to receive your spouse back when they are ready to turn from their sin. Allow Jesus to prepare your heart for reconciliation.

If my children are doing something harmful or destructive, I don't have any problem correcting them and steering their bad choices in a healthier direction. It's correction born out of love. I don't hold malice towards my kids when I let them know their actions are unacceptable. I love them enough to teach them the right way. I should have the same level of concern for my husband.

If I stomp around the house entertaining a pity party, or I make stupid choices, I expect Glen to say something to bring me back to my senses. It seems natural that he would say something, because he is not afraid of speaking the truth plainly.

Those who steer away from confrontation, (like yours truly) can't seem to convince themselves that pointing their mate in a healthy direction is good. Halting bad behavior is actually a peaceful way to operate. I cringe at the idea of standing up for myself and telling Glen he is wrong, I would rather have a root canal. I tend to allow things that hurt me to go on for years, before I finally break down and talk about it. I have found though, that when I make myself draw a line and say, "When you do this it hurts me," or "When this happens, I feel like…" we both understand the issue more clearly. When I force myself to approach touchy subjects in a reasonable manner, I usually have great payoffs. Glen is open to hear my needs and suggestions when I respectfully explain my point of view. I used to have to be at my wit's end before I could say anything. By then I was really angry, and it all came out with way more emotion than was needed. Remaining calm puts us in an honorable position of reasoning.

If your spouse is habitually wounding and sacrificing your marriage, such as being in an unrepentant affair, it is completely appropriate to say in a calm voice "I will not allow you to do this anymore." While doing this, remember the verse: "A gentle answer turns away wrath, but a harsh word stirs up anger." (Proverbs 15:1 NAS) Screaming and throwing a fit only puts the focus on your inability to control yourself. Soft and deliberate words, directed with care, focus the attention on the original issue.

If there is never a consequence to sin, there is usually no sense in stopping the sin. Seriously, if I could eat peanut butter cups all day and never gain a pound, you better believe I would eat them. I would go bankrupt on candy bars, but there is a high price to pay for indulging the flesh.

It's the same with unfaithfulness. I would encourage anyone who has a spouse in unrepentant sexual sin to find a counselor, a pastor, a close friend or relative who can give wise counsel. Preferably, find someone who wants to see healing for both of you. Don't ask the neighbor who is on a fourth marriage, or the irritable boss who has never been married. Look for someone whom you know has a successful marriage or at least a positive outlook on marriage. Ask them to help you determine what steps you can take to steer your mate's destructive actions toward healthy behaviors. Help, or encourage, your spouse to find someone to be accountable to.

Treat this as a disease or illness that needs immediate attention. If you would do this for your children, why wouldn't you show the same concern for your marriage partner? Is it because you are too offended by the sin? If so, remember that you promised on your wedding day to love and honor. Loving and honoring means setting aside your own feelings to serve the other. Placing your spouse's needs before your own is the truest kind of love. Your spouse needs help, and chances are that spouse will have a difficult time seeking counsel.

Glen was accountable to many people. Since we had been in a ministry leadership role, and he had to confess to so many friends, his "audience" was much larger than average. One would think that would be enough, but when the Lord moved us to new places, a new church, and new areas of responsibility, Glen made sure that the leadership knew of our past. It was his decision. I had felt so badly about making him confess to our family, our church, and our marriage ministry leadership couples; but when I no longer asked that of him, he volunteered it on his own. This has been amazing to me. When he was asked to serve on our church board, he went to the pastor and told him our story, so that any ounce of deceit would be squelched. How beautifully this demonstrates the effects of loving discipline.

Know that God is working to honor your marriage covenant even more than either of you are. All through the Old Testament, covenants were formed. Some were kept and some were broken. Repeated instances of blessing were poured out on those who remained faithful to covenant. Consequences were obvious to those who broke covenant. God desires to see your marriage healed. He doesn't just want to see you obeying; He wants to pour out blessings on your home. "The Lord preserves the faithful"…Psalm 31:23 (NAS)

ARE WE SURVIVORS?

Our story happened in 1996. It has been long enough now that as we look back, we seem far away from that difficult time. Life has gone on, our children are growing, and our ministry was restored. God, in His mercy, has allowed us to use what the enemy meant for destruction, for God's glory. We are able to share with other couples that there is restoration available to them even in the worst of situations. We certainly haven't "arrived." But our unity is stronger than ever, our love grows daily, our desire to be with each other flourishes, and our hearts are tender towards the other.

I feel more loved by Glen than I ever thought possible. He has shown me devotion during sickness, financial struggle, growing older, and life's ups and downs. It wasn't anything I could have possibly made him do myself. It required an act of creating, an act of God, in both of us.

God created in us a heart of love for each other. Our ability to reach out to each other has increased more and more as we continue to learn how to be focused on the other's needs, rather than our own. The more we fulfill each other, the more we ourselves find fulfillment.

God blessed us with another daughter in 2001. Her middle name is Dawn which to us represents a new day and a new beginning. We truly have been given a new beginning. Our respect for each other is so much stronger. It is like we are living a brand new life. Accusations and expectations are being replaced with gratefulness for who the other is. We find fulfillment in teaching together, hanging around together, and doing life side-by-side.

Usually when I see a "crop" in Glen's life that I don't like, I can trace it back to seed that I myself have sown in him. If it's growing, someone planted it there. Weeds can only be uprooted with decisive pulling and effort. We have to be on the lookout for our own responsibility in every matter.

We still have to pay careful attention not to let outside influences dilute the purity of what God has done. Television, radio, computers, billboards, and images of provocatively dressed people all have to be in constant check. We are certainly not immune to sin. Keeping a handle on what is fed into our marriage is a key to protecting our hearts.

Glen has open freedom to say "Honey, can you stand between me and the woman in that mini skirt so I don't have her right in front of my face." He knows he can ask me that, and I won't judge him for temptation.

I know that if I am around a tender man who attracts me with his personality, it is just as dangerous for me. I know I have the freedom to tell Glen I am in trouble with my own wandering eye.

The really cool thing for me is that as I see Glen walking beyond what happened, and living victoriously, he is more attractive to me than anyone or anything. He is my hero in many ways. I had no idea I could love him so deeply.

When he shares our testimony, I am swept away with love for him.

When we see other couples begin to experience healing, it fires us up! It's like this incredible fountain of forgiveness, that all we have to do is dip into it and drink, then power surges through us. When we get to share the bubbling fountain with others, it's an awesome celebration. Our tears of joy stream unashamedly as we listen to couple after couple share their own stories of God's redeeming grace.

So, are we survivors? "No. In all these things we are more than conquerors through Christ who loved us." (Rom. 8:37 NIV)

If you are reading this because you find yourself on this same journey, please know that although this is not an easy road, it is a passable road. Take the hand of your Heavenly Father and hold on tight. He will never leave you, and he will never forsake you. He has healing just up the road, if you will follow His instructions. He loves you so much! He is faithful. He is faithful when all else fails and everyone else fails you. He is the One True Friend that sticks closer than a brother (Proverbs 18:24.) Let Him guide you over the rocks and around the turns ahead. He already knows the way, and He is waiting to show that way to you and your spouse, too. We have tried Him and found him trustworthy. When there is no one left to trust, trust Him. It's alright, He is safe.

Allow him to turn this disaster in your life into your own victory. Some day you will turn to another and say, "God is faithful; He will bring you to restoration. I know, because He did it for me!"

Conclusion

On the next pages, you will find a summary of some of the key points that were tucked away in each chapter of our story. I have highlighted these points with illustrations to bring to your remembrance some of the major turning points in our lives.

I also included some of the points for an unrepentant spouse, since in our ministry we have seen how these can help as well. All roads to restoration may not be identical. You may find these steps need to come in a different order for your situation, or you may be directed to add or subtract things to fit your own story.

It may be necessary for you to review these illustrations or re-read the book when you are farther down the road to healing. Just as we need to take more than one look at a map when we are traveling, you may need to re-check the directions on your journey as well.

It is my sincere desire that your broken heart be mended. The transformation from victim to victor is not an easy one. You will need to stay focused on your goal to reach wholeness. Thankfully, when we make a wrong turn, Jesus is ever ready to set our feet back on the road to victory.

1. Give God control of your reactions and ask Him to steer your life so that it may be healed. This can, and should be done right away.

2. Forgive right away, even when you don't feel like it. Feelings will come later. This is not excusing the offense, but rather taking control of your will before bitterness begins to control you.

3. If your spouse is repentant, stay together so that you can work through the issues together. Let this become a team effort.

4. Contact a Spiritually mature couple or individual who will help you both work toward healing. Find someone who will help you focus on mending your marriage, rather than someone who will take sides.

5. Don't fall into the trap of deceit. The sin needs to be exposed to someone who will hold you accountable. The offender needs to know that there is a cost of exposure, and the offended needs to be accountable for not embracing bitterness.

6. If your spouse is unrepentant, pray for wisdom on how to set boundaries. Allowing the bad behavior to continue without consequence, and expecting to see a change, is unrealistic. Seek counsel for establishing a non-vindictive response when sinful actions occur. Stay calm, firm and consistent in drawing the boundary line.

7. If you choose to separate, do it with the understanding that this is not for the end result of divorce, but for the destructive behavior to cease. Expect repentance to happen and you will not be surprised when it does. Keep your heart ready to reconcile when repentance comes.

8. Set a reasonable goal for returning to regular daily life and ministry. Give yourself a chance to grieve, and don't begrudge your healing time; but don't allow yourself to wallow in self-pity for years afterwards either.

9. In spite of your wounded heart, try to recognize your spouses' efforts and praise them for trying to work on the marriage.

10. Allow the offending spouse to confess the entire depth of sin. Ask God for wisdom in how much detail you should know, but give permission for the whole truth to come out unless God counsels you otherwise. This will keep you from repeated wounding as you find out new truths after the initial shock. Forgive again and again after each new truth is revealed. Don't allow the barbs of resentment to take hold.

11. If you are the offender, it is EXTREMELY IMPORTANT that you confess the extent of your sin when your spouse asks for it. It may seem you are protecting them from further trauma by not telling the whole truth, but it will seem like another lie when they find out there's more. The road to healing is severely damaged when your partner has to reopen the wound and begin healing again with each new revelation of offense. Better to only have to mend it once, than to have to repeatedly tear and heal.

12. If the outside relationship is not yet ended, cut it off abruptly. Don't try to ease away from it. Make a call together, if possible, and let the other person know you are both on the line. Establish the fact that there will be no more contact. Offer forgiveness, but be firm in your desire to exclude them from any further involvement in your lives. Pray together afterwards as husband and wife for God to cut the emotional attachment that was created by the extra-marital relationship.

13. Don't allow even the smallest amount of deceit to creep back in. Keep your marriage pure. Be aware that you both may be tempted to sin again.

14. Make it a new habit to talk and pray together at least once each day. This is crucial for connecting in the Spirit and the Soul realms. We are three part beings: Spirit, soul and body. Discover what a 3-D relationship looks like if you have been living in 2-D. Even if it's only a minute or two each day, make the time for this prayer connection.

15. Ask God to show you any areas that He needs to change in you, even if you are the betrayed spouse. Check for any areas in your thinking that are motivated by selfishness.

16. Look for "treasures" in your spouse; things that you love about them. Point them out to your spouse as well as highlighting them in your own mind.

17. If you are the offender, apologize as often as your spouse needs to hear it. Assure them that your heart is truly repentant and you are not just sorry you were caught. They need to know that your sorrow over the past gives you determination to avoid temptation in the future.

18. If you are the offended, don't abuse your mate's willingness to apologize. Don't repeat their sins back to them, using them as a weapon.

19. Return to the sexual union with care. The wounded spouse may need a lot of grace in tackling mental images. It may be necessary to take this in steps and back off when hurtful memories surface. Woo the heart back into security and the body should follow. If intimacy doesn't return within several months, you may need to seek help. Try praying together before love-making. It may sound odd, but it can be a powerful healing balm. Make sure this area of your marriage does not get neglected (remember, 3-D not 2-D. Spirit- Soul- Body.)

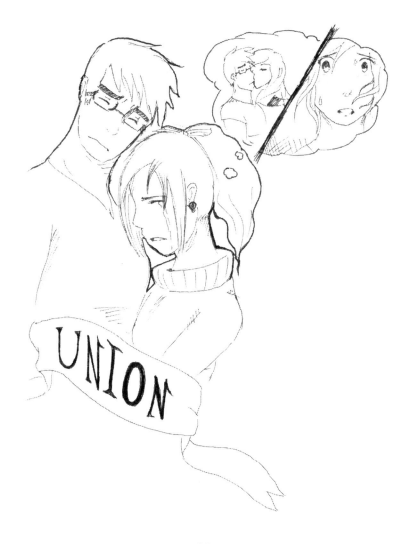

20. Remember that it is not a sin to have thought your spouse innocent when they were guilty. It is a sin to accuse your spouse when they are innocent. Be your mate's intercessor and not their accuser.

21. As time brings out effects of sin that surface in new areas, keep in mind that a new sin hasn't occurred. Remind yourself that the new damage you find is another "leg" of the original sin. Many, if not all, areas of your life will naturally be altered by traumatic circumstances. These repair and adjustment times are a part of rebuilding.

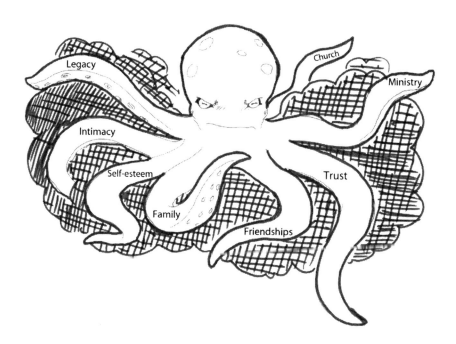

22. Review Biblical verses on forgiveness. Put your names in where they apply. (The chapter on "Creating a Good Habit" will help you get started with this.) Repeat these Scriptures to yourself, and anyone you feel may support you, or who would benefit from them as well.

23. Share with others how God is healing you. This will help solidify it to them, and to you. When others see you making progress they will be more willing to cheer you on. Your testimony of healing may help another marriage get through a difficult time.

ACKNOWLEDGMENTS

I am grateful to our son, David, our daughter, Kristi, and our friend, Ben Campbell, for illustrating these points in a fun and real way. God has wonderfully given us supportive family and friends with servant hearts.

I am truly thankful for my parents, Pastor Tom and Ginger Blackburn, who not only helped me in the recovery process in my marriage, but who also spent many hours helping me edit and put together this book.

Glen, I can not thank you enough for your support and encouragement. This is a brave and admirable step for you. I know this brings risk and exposure to you; yet you have not swayed in your determination that this material needs to get out for the help of others. I am honored to be doing life with you. Your willingness to back me up, in every way, is touching to my heart. You have truly won me back to you. "Until death do us part," is a comfort and a joy now. I love you!

Laura Samuelson's ministries have included serving as a youth group leader, women's ministry leader, crisis pregnancy counselor, and retreat speaker. She and her husband, Glen, teach marriage, engagement, and parenting classes and seminars. Parents of five children, they live in Garden City, Idaho.

CPSIA information can be obtained at www.ICGtesting.com
Printed in the USA
LVOW08s2232070814

398029LV00002BA/440/P